Peggy Rooney is the Author of:

- ~ Uncommon Conversations with God
- ~ The Ant Hills
- ~ Prisms of the Soul
- ~ In Search of the Songbird
- ~ To Rome with Love:
  Cardinal James Hickey
- ~ Love Letters to Anna
- ~ What I Did on My Summer Vacations, or
  "What Did I Say That God Didn't Like?"
- ~ The Torchbearers
- ~ Finding God in Everyday Miracles
- ~ The Tree House
- ~ Poetry in Shadows and in Splendor

Balancing Life on the Edge of a Cliff

Chapter Table of Contents Page

1 The Sunset 4
2 The Awakening 8
3 Changing Worlds 13
4 Answered Prayers 18
5 Life's Many Surprises 24
6 Poor Little Princess 29
7 Childhood Memories 34
8 Ms. Rooney, Take a Letter 38
9 On the Job Training 44
10 The Tap Root 50
11 A Place Called Home 57
12 Shifting Times 63
13 The Revolving Job Doors 70
14 The Sproutland 77
15 Grow Where You Are Planted 83
16 The Confrontation 90
17 Mountains Are for Moving 94
18 The Threads of Life 101
19 Cast Your Bread Upon the Waters 108
20 Life Is Change 116
21 The Cardinal's Good Humor 121
22 Serendipities 125
23 My Lucky Break 128
24 Signs of Hope 133
25 Healing Trip 136
26 The Cardinal's Health Challenges 140
27 The Greatest of These Is Love 145

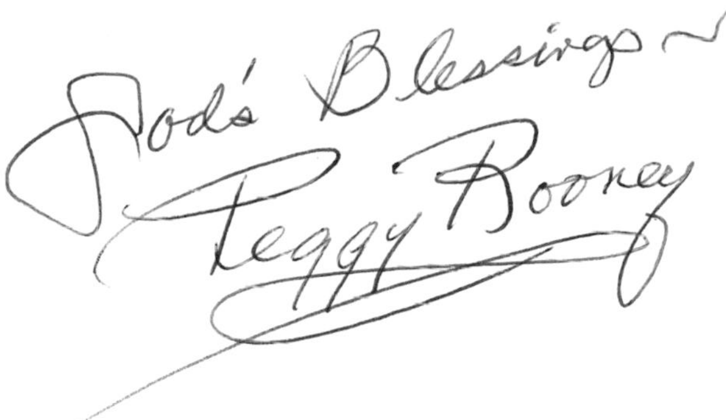

Balancing Life on the Edge of a Cliff

Creating a balance in life is imperative, for living on the edge of a cliff can be a frightening place. We realize the dangers we face by cliffhanging, and often it is only in reaching out to God that we are rescued from the fall.

****

This memoir is a rewritten version of my book The Ant Hills, and is a more comprehensive rendering of my story.

prmuses@verizon.net

Dedication

Balancing Life on the Edge of a Cliff is dedicated to the many people who are learning that even though life can be uncertain, there is a Divine Power ready to guide us off the cliff's edge.

Acknowledgement

I give much appreciation to Debralee Lyndon for designing the book's creative cover.

I wish to thank Walter Gilbert for again offering his guidance and expertise in preparing my book for print.

I also wish to thank Donna Knott for her invaluable help in guiding me through the publishing process.

Finding God in Everyday Miracles

I know miracles occur, because I've experienced miracles often in my life, but that's not to say that all we have to do is to ask God for a miracle and he will comply. Miracles often emerge as an answer to prayer, but sometimes we receive a miracle when we least expect it, as a message from God, giving us hope. He knows that hope is our link to him and that we need hope to lift our spirits. Hope helps our faith in God to grow.

There are times, however, when hope for the future seems grim, when suffering makes life so difficult that it's hard to hold on to hope. Where is God when our desperate prayers go unanswered? We lose heart at those times. Our worst fears manifest and we wonder how to reach God and why he has failed us. When this happens, clarity is lost. We are filled with doubts and fears. We mourn our loses.

God sometimes uses those hard times to redirect our lives so that when our world stops trembling, he can guide us on a new path. But at other times, tragedy can only be explained by accepting God's mysteries. Of course, we question these deep tragedies, especially when we have prayed so long and so deeply for answers. Those are the times when only faith can carry us forward. *God's plans are not always our plans.*

What is a miracle? The dictionary defines a miracle as a "supernatural act." The dictionary also defines supernatural act as "outside the laws of nature." I cannot prove my everyday miracles have been supernatural acts, or that they are outside the laws of nature. I can only say that when they occur, I feel my life has been touched by God in a profound way. They help guide my actions and give me visual hope as I witness the power of miracles. While there are occurrences in my life which seem to defy answers, God often speaks to me through an *everyday miracle*, giving me hope.

Miracles can be great or small, so small that we often miss them. I'd like to share some of my miracles and the lessons life has taught me. As I take you through my personal struggles, know that it is imperative to create balance in life. Living on the *edge of a cliff* can be a frightening place. We realize the dangers we face by cliffhanging, and often, it is only in reaching out to God that we are rescued from the fall.

Some miracles were given to me as a gift of hope. But when my miracles were arranged as stepping stones to a better life, they were so visual that even my friends would say they must be a gift from God. I hope you see God's hand in these stepping stones, and that they help to recall your own *everyday miracles*.

The wooded area bordering my grandparents' home was my favorite corner of the world as a child. On warm spring days I would crouch on a blanket of moss and watch in fascination as tiny ants labored to build their cone-like homes. Often their hard work was trampled by prowling feet and I wondered what motivated these small creatures to rebuild — to push and haul and go forward at all odds toward their destiny. Years later, I would recall this memory as I struggled toward my own destiny. Like those tiny ants, I *pushed* and *hauled* to rebuild my life, only to have my dreams trampled by "prowling feet."

I married in my teens and, for twenty-one years, lived a cloistered and demeaning life. There were no shelters or advocates for women in that era, and those in authority would not intervene in domestic disputes. I had no where to turn.

Then, one spring night, life, as I had known it, ended abruptly. The full impact of my actions confronted me as I stood at the door of a convent with two of my four children, begging the nuns for help. There was no turning back. I was homeless, with no transportation, no job or job experience and, in my pocket, our only means of support — seven crumpled dollar bills and some change.

In my desperate leap for survival, I ran headlong into the fears and self-doubts I had eluded for so long. In the glare of the convent's street lights, those doubts and fears hovered like luminous demons, challenging my decision and taunting me with my perceived inability to survive in a world I hardly knew.

I was not aware of it at the time, but casting out those demons would lead toward an adventure that would recreate me again and again. In facing the demons, I found the strength and courage to abandon the familiar and to allow myself to be reinvented by life's struggles, but always asking the question — *why the prowling feet came so often to trample my dreams*? Over the years, I have journeyed from survival to healing in my search for God and the answer to that question.

Chapter 1 **The Sunset**

Looking back, I can see where the transforming era of the explosive sixties took me psychologically through the same changes that had devastated our nation. So much was happening around me. The civil rights movement was in earnest, the assassinations of both President John Kennedy and his brother Robert Kennedy, and Martin Luther King's murder in 1968.

Television gave us the image of the first lunar landing. I seemed to be experiencing a death of my own and somewhere on the horizon I, too, wanted to travel through time and space, someplace far from home. The `60s propelled me into the early `70s with forceful changes within my inner spirit.

It had been a turbulent evening. I was tired, with little energy to defend myself. Suddenly, I was thrust out of the house, the front door locked behind me. I remember feeling a surge of numbness through my body, along with a deep sense of humiliation. I stared at the small window frames connecting the panes of glass in the front door. They reminded me of prison bars. Something snapped inside me. The words, *never again*, ran through my head like a mantra. Then, as if a stranger had taken possession of my body, I raised both hands, doubled them into tight fists and hurled them through two panes of glass. I reached in, unlocking the door, and walked stiffly back into the house. Confusion washed over me as I wondered what I should do next. Pulling my coat down from the hook in the kitchen, I left the house again through the back door, dripping blood from my cuts.

I walked toward the lights of the shopping center, feeling a deep anguish churning in the pit of my stomach. I thought I might be sick. I had no idea where I was headed. Through swelling tears, I noticed two policemen sitting in a parked cruiser. Over the years, I had been told that the police could not become involved in domestic affairs. What they were really saying was that when a woman takes a vow of obedience in marriage, as women did in those times, she is subject to her husband's control. To my surprise, however, the two policemen agreed to go into my home while I gathered my children and our belongings. It felt like a miracle. After all those years, someone in authority was willing to help me.

Joe, my six-year-old son, clasped the hem of my coat as I struggled through the front door with two suitcases. I noticed that someone had left a glass of milk sitting on the coffee table. With a sudden reflex, I sat the bags down to empty it. I picked them up again. What did it matter?

In those days, women didn't discuss trouble in the family and as I walked toward the taxi where my daughter Debralee was already waiting, I vaguely wondered if the neighbors were staring from their windows. I shoved the suitcases into the waiting cab and slid across the seat, pulling Joe into the cab with me. I felt that deep sense of humiliation again, especially for my children. But before I could take a breath, Joe leaped from the taxi and bolted up the front steps of the house. Confused, and not wanting to relive the exodus, I waited.

Moments later, Joe appeared in the doorway of the house carrying two shopping bags brimming with stuffed animals and dragging a five-foot stuffed frog behind him. He struggled down the concrete steps, through the white picket gate and, with tears coasting down his cheeks, jostled his menagerie into the taxi. He moved across the seat and nestled close to me, swallowing muffled sobs and tightly clutching what was left of his world. One of the shopping bags had bold lettering with the holiday greeting — *Merry Christmas.* At that moment it seemed absurd.

"Look, lady," the taxi driver blurted out impatiently, "where to?" He stared at me through the rear view mirror, waiting for an answer. I stared back uncomfortably. I had no idea *where to.* He repeated questioning, "You called the cab, lady, don't you have somewhere you wanna go?"

What was I going to do? I had no place to go, no car or job, a taxicab full of debris, and two of my children. Who would want us? After a few seconds, I heard myself say, "Take us to the convent at Mount Calvary Church." So with that, the taxi driver turned the cab around and headed for the main highway. We drove away from the familiar into a tunnel of darkness, the soft red hue of the May sunset dying on the road behind us. "God, if you really hear prayers, hear me now," I whispered. "Tell me what I'm to do next?"

I was numb. I could feel nothing ... except fear. How would I support us? I had never worked a full-time job and had no skills. Who would hire me? I wasn't at all certain about what I had just done. I had lived in an abusive situation out of fear, seemingly unequipped to escape the demons that ruled my life. I realized at that moment that the unknown can also be a fearful place to live. Fear is so strong an emotion that even when you've shut down on your feelings, fear seeps through. My fears and insecurities were so strong that night I thought they might destroy me. Somewhere inside, you know when you've crossed the line into the unknown; that place you were so afraid of facing. You're not exactly certain how it happened, but something emerges inside that you weren't even aware of. It takes on a life of its own and you realize you've just experienced the end of an era.

The taxi swung around to the side door of the convent. I paid the fare and we stumbled out of the cab, dragging our possessions behind us. I pressed the doorbell and heard it buzz inside the convert, announcing our arrival. My heart was pounding. The outside light snapped on and I felt as if a spotlight had just streaked across the black sky, stripping away all of my armor.

I saw faces peering from the side window and wondered if this had been such a good idea. We must have been a strange sight in the flood of the porch lamp; a disheveled woman, a teenage girl staring into space like a wooden puppet, a little boy with dirt-streaked face, twenty-seven stuffed animals — that by now had broken through the tattered bags — and a purple and green five-foot frog.

The door opened and the sisters rushed out to meet us. They were wearing bathrobes and had removed their head veils, obviously not expecting visitors. The thought ran through my mind that I wasn't the only one without a facade. Debralee stared at them with a look of shocked reality. The year was 1971 and the nuns still wore the traditional habit. She had been a student at the school during her elementary years and had never seen the nuns without their veils. An age-old question was answered for me that night as I thought, *my god — they do have hair.*

One of the nuns helped gather up Joe's stuffed animals. "All of you must be cold," she said sympathetically. "Come in where it's warm." So the good sisters took us in and for the next three weeks the convent became our sanctuary.

#####

In the taxi, on the way to the convent, I was lost in thought about the child in me who was once so brave. At an early age, I sought out opportunities to flex my courage. I would climb to the top of the highest tree in the neighborhood, then wrap my fingers around the top limb and swing as I had seen circus performers swaying on a trapeze. I had no fear.

Where was that child now? Had I abandoned her along the way? Perhaps she was buried somewhere inside me. I would spend the next few years searching for her.

Chapter 2 **The Awakening**

That night, in the dim light of a strange bedroom, all the confusion of the evening paraded before me like dark silhouettes on the wall. It felt as if I had awakened from a bout of insanity. I no longer understood who I was. I had been a wife, a homemaker, and the mother of four. Now, life was fragmented, my family scattered. In the protection of the convent, I was free to think my own thoughts without fear of reprisal. But there was another fear — fear of the world outside the convert walls. What was waiting for me? I couldn't think too far into the future. I instinctively knew that before I could reason with life, I must begin the healing process, and before the healing, I needed to grieve. I wondered if re-entering the world would allow time for grieving.

What a terrible time in my daughter Kathy's life. She was to graduate from high school within weeks. I had envisioned that moment as a happy celebration. Instead, it would always stand out as a dark moment in our lives. To complete her last few weeks of high school, Kathy stayed with a friend who lived within walking distance of school.

In the haste of leaving our home that night, I had packed Johnny's clothes, but his father pulled him aside and pleaded with him not to leave. His father had never given him the attention he gave to his little brother, so it must have been affirming to have his father single him out and say he needed him. Johnny, who had celebrated his ninth birthday two days before, hesitated at first, then said he would stay. I feel sure now that he didn't understand that we weren't coming back. I was numb. The policemen told me that, because of Johnny's age, I would have him back with me in a matter of weeks with legal counsel. Now, having asserted myself, I knew it would be a disaster to stay in the house once the police left.

My spirit seemed to parallel the apprehension of the `70s. It was a time when our nation doubted the future. I had those same doubts about my personal outlook.

That first night in the convent, lying in the shadow of the crucifix above my bed, I wanted to roll up into a fetal position and shut out the world, but I prayed for strength and guidance. I soaked in the serenity, letting it permeate my spirit, hoping for healing. I knew that all too quickly the world would come to drag me out into the stark light of reality. In those days, there were no shelters or women's groups to help fight for the rights of a woman.

Joe was young enough to adapt easily to our newfound home. He loved all the attention from the sisters, and they welcomed the liveliness of this effusive child who ran through the long hallways bellowing, "mom!" He reveled in being allowed to choose a different shower stall each morning from among twenty-five.

One morning, while Joe played in the shower with a balloon he had found in his pants pocket, the balloon suddenly deflated, slipping from his grip and slithering down the drainpipe. I was horrified. What if it ruined the plumbing? After Joe dressed and we went downstairs to breakfast, I confessed to Mother Superior about the balloon's disappearance. I expected her to be aggravated when I asked, "Do you think the balloon will stop up the pipes?"

"I don't know," she said serenely, "we've never had a balloon in the drainpipes."

Each night at the supper meal, Joe would drag Freddie, the five-foot frog, into the dining room and prayers would be delayed while Joe got Freddie into position to pray. Freddie was taller than Joe and three times as round. "Come on, Freddie," he'd command, "now stand up and put your hands together, we're gonna pray," he would coax. By some miracle, Freddie would finally behave like a good Catholic frog and prayers would proceed.

Debralee was going through an emotional crisis and although

relieved to have the safe harbor of the convent, she kept to herself. She listened intently to what was being said during the evenings when everyone gathered in the community room, but offered little conversation of her own.

Johnny was a student at the parish school, so each day during recess I stood on the playground, waiting to see him. During those three weeks, I watched him change from a happy, animated little boy to a morose, distant child. He was pulling away more each day. Being a mother had been my life and I was a good mother, but I was losing him.

One evening, standing out back of the convent, I heard a car drive up. I turned to see my husband behind the wheel, Johnny sitting in the back seat. He had found us. There was a violent outburst and the nuns rushed out from the convent to help. Johnny never looked up during the confusion that followed. It was as if we were invisible to him, but as the car pulled away, the street light fell across the back window and a sad face turned to stare at me, a small hand timidly raised, waving goodbye. I didn't know it then, but it was goodbye — goodbye to the nine-year-old I loved so much. I would soon discover that often court proceedings are slow and judges don't always care. How could I lose my child when all I had done was to fight for my life?

That night, while my two children slept in the protection of the convent, I slipped out the kitchen door and into the church. I loved the church. I had converted to Catholicism at the age of twenty-nine after attending Mass for some years with my husband's family. There was a sense of God's mystery about the Mass that appealed to my inner life. I had found a spiritual home, but I was still searching for a personal relationship with the entity I called God. I knelt in the darkened pew and admitted how frightened and insecure I felt.

When a woman lives with oppression long enough, her feelings of anguish and grief distort her self-knowledge. I was fighting to discover who I was. I knew I was worth more than mere existence. I sobbed until my throat ached and begged God to give me a sign so I would know I had done the right thing. “Send me the help I need,” I pleaded.

The week before we left the convent, we got a ride to Kathy’s school for her graduation. I was proud of her as she walked across the stage to accept her diploma. I was equally proud of the way she pulled her life together under such terrible circumstances. She already had a job in Virginia and was to move into a tiny apartment close to her job. If Kathy could begin a new life in spite of all the frustration, surely I could do the same.

I had found an oasis at the convent, a place where nothing could touch me — a place of peace. But after three weeks, I knew I had to give up my sanctuary and begin a new life. It frightened me. In fact, I was terrified. I would have to make some hard decisions — to find a job and a place to live. I would have to face cold reality whether I was ready for it or not.

Our farewells were spotted with tears the day we left the convent, but my heart overflowed with gratitude for all the good sisters had done for us. The warmth and security I had found with these caring women gave me a sturdy beginning to a new life and would remain one of my fondest memories.

#####

I remember as a small child of four, leaving the safe harbor of my grandparents’ home where I was living, to visit my mother on occasional weekends. She lived on the top floor of a row house in Washington, D.C. That particular weekend, after dinner, she opened a package and took out a book of Jeanette McDonald paper dolls and some small scissors she had bought for me. She said she was only going down the street for a little while with friends and asked me to sit on the floor and cut out the paper dolls. She told me that by the time I was finished, she would be back.

After I had cut them out and played for a while, I remember going to the window and peering out at the street below. Although I wasn't afraid, I remember feeling lost. I wanted to go home, but I didn't know where home was.

Maybe this was what I felt now — lost — wanting to go home. I watched from the taxicab window as the neighborhoods sped by, and I wondered where home was.

Chapter 3 **Changing Worlds**

My mother had lived in Los Angeles for twenty years, but moved back to the East Coast a few months earlier. She recently rented a one-room, efficiency apartment in Greenbelt, a small suburb of Maryland. From the convent, we went to her tiny apartment with the few possessions we owned; only now I had an added item — a second-hand bicycle someone had given me — my first means of transportation.

It was dreadfully hot the day we moved in. With no air conditioning in my mother's tiny apartment, it was dreadfully humid, giving us a vigorous sense of togetherness.

"Where am I sleeping?" Debralee moaned.

"Right there on the floor with the rest of us," I said, "between the table and the bicycle."

"But I don't have any place to put my clothes," she complained.

"You don't have that many," I said. "You can keep them folded on the chair."

Joe yelled, "Mom, I'm hungry!"

"That's okay, Joe, we're going to the grocery store in the morning." My mother lived on a very limited income, so I knew I would have to shop for groceries with the little money I had left — less than five dollars.

That night, lying on the floor between the table and the bicycle, I was feeling pretty desperate and tears came quickly. How do I begin? I needed a job and a place to live. We had left so much behind in the thunder of parting. My heart ached for my son, John, and I missed Kathy. There was so much insecurity surrounding our separations. We were all living in a fragmented world without any continuity to our lives. In the silence of the night, my fears loomed like clattering ghosts. I wanted to wail but, instead, muffled my sobs with the woolly teddy bear I was using for a pillow. I felt as if all the fire, the passion, and the will to endure had gone out of me.

I needed a job quickly and applied the next day at the local grocery food chain. I figured the grocery store was within bicycling distance from my mother's apartment and, I reasoned, working as a cashier would get me out among people again. But deep down inside I also knew there was another reason. I had little confidence in my abilities. I was sure no one else would hire me.

All that week, I waited anxiously for a phone call telling me my job application had been accepted. It never came. One morning, having ridden my bicycle to the store, I overheard a cashier say she had given her notice and would be leaving in a week. I was excited. I hurried back to the apartment to phone the personnel manager.

"Mr. Stanley, this is Peggy Rooney," I introduced myself. "I understand there will be an opening for a cashier in the Greenbelt store. I have an application on file and I'd like that job."

He laughed. "Do you know how many people are waiting for that job? I'd say twenty-five are ahead of you, but there might be a possible opening soon at one of our other locations."

I knew the distances involved in working at other locations. "Mr. Stanley, I really need *that* job. You don't understand," I pressed. "I have to work in Greenbelt. You see, Mr. Stanley, I only have a bicycle and can't get any further!" There must have been a touch of desperation in my voice. After a long pause he said, "Okay, that's a good reason. You've got the job."

So the following week I reported for work at 9:00 a.m. The first question I was asked when I arrived was, "Where did you park?"

"On the parking lot," I answered.

"No, no...you'll have to move it to the street."

"But it's only a bicycle," I told him. Well, that seemed to strike everyone humorously. "Hey," he shouted, "she rides a bike to work!" And everyone laughed.

Little did he know, the bike was my one possession in life.

My new job was physically tiring and I was on my feet all day. Through wind and rain, I pedaled my bike the four-mile round-trip to and from work each day, but I was grateful to have a job.

A few weeks on the job, I got a quick lesson in the perils of being a single woman in the work world. I was told that the most I could expect to work was twenty hours a week. So to be offered more hours meant a lot to me.

As the store opened one morning, I stood at the register waiting for the customers to wheel their carts over and pile the groceries onto the conveyer belt. Larry, an intense man with a thick mustache and darting eyes, came down from the office and walked over to my counter. He smiled pleasantly. I smiled back.

"How're you doing?" he asked.

"I'm doing just fine," I answered.

"I hear you're trying to make it on your own. Must be rough."

"A little," I admitted.

"How would you like to have more hours here at the store?"

"I'd love it," I tossed back, thinking how nice it was of him to be concerned.

"Great!" he declared. "I can arrange it for you."

"Are you sure?" I questioned. "That would be wonderful!"

"It's no problem. All you have to do is meet me after work some evening at a motel on Route I."

I stared at him blankly, feeling the heat of humiliation stinging my face. I didn't want to jeopardize my job by an angry outburst and I wasn't going to let him know how vulnerable I felt. Finally, I managed, "No, Larry, I really can't do that, but it doesn't matter — you'd probably just be disappointed anyway."

He looked at me curiously for a brief second, then turned and walked away. He never asked me again, and I kept my twenty hours a week. Although Congress had just passed the Equal Rights Amendment, I was still waiting for my emancipation, not yet realizing that I had the power to liberate myself.

I was grateful for the refuge of my mother's tiny apartment, but I knew it was time to search for a place of our own. I canvassed the neighborhood for days until I was exhausted. It was discouraging. There were either no vacancies, I couldn't afford the rent, or they wouldn't allow children.

One scorching afternoon, exhausted from walking, I stopped at a store for a cold soda. I was standing at the back of the store sipping my drink and feeling pretty sorry for myself when, just at eye level, I noticed a small, handwritten sign on the bulletin board. It read: APARTMENT TO SUBLET THRU OCTOBER. Excitedly, I scribbled the phone number on a piece of paper and hurried back to my mother's apartment to call.

From the other end of the phone I heard a woman say she had rented the place to a couple only that morning. "Just let me come over," I pressed. "Maybe they'll change their minds." For some reason, she agreed. I couldn't believe this was really non-assertive me talking. It's strange what happens inside you when circumstances press you into action.

I fell in love with the tiny place. It was a small efficiency with a plastic covered, pullout sofa in the living room. Against one wall nestled a petite kitchen where you could cook, wash dishes and scrub the floor without ever moving from one spot. There was a small bathroom, and a tiny separate bedroom with a "real" bed. I wanted that bed! All evening I held the thought that the couple would decide against taking the apartment. That was my first attempt at what is now called visualization. It worked. At eight o'clock that night the phone rang. The couple had decided not to take the apartment after all. Was I still interested? The bed was mine, even if I had to share it with Joe, twenty-seven stuffed animals, and Freddie, the five-foot frog!

We moved in that week. We had our own a temporary home, complete with black asphalt flooring that never looked clean, casement windows that leaked when it rained, stained walls, and furniture that smelled like a soggy muskrat. It was beautiful!

#####

When I started first grade, my life changed abruptly. My mother wanted me to come live with her during the school year. I began staying with my grandparents on weekends and during summer vacations. One of the drawbacks was that my mother moved around a lot. Sometimes I would change schools each year. I became good at making quick adjustments but, because of these moves, I was never able to make lasting friendships at school or in the neighborhood. Life became lonely. Change was something I soon learned to dislike and fear. It still frightened me.

Chapter 4 **Answered Prayers**

I awoke one morning to autumn's impatient entry. It swirled on gale winds, ripping the aging leaves from their bearings and tossing them irritably to the ground. Watching this assault from my window, I realized that we would soon be forced out of our little efficiency into the autumn wind — but where? Money was a problem. Even if I could afford the rent on an apartment, I had no money for the initial costs of the first month's rent plus the security deposit. I was not a good credit risk, having job security of only three months, and I had no cosigner to help ensure my credit stability. As I watched the leaves playfully chasing each other, I could feel the fears I'd stuffed down inside me fighting their way back, assaulting my peace of mind like the autumn wind.

I thought of the home I had left behind. At this time of year, I would be gathering up the tools to rake the yard and cover the plants from the cold. I loved my home. I did not want to leave it. It was the home my grandparents had built after moving to Maryland, the home where I grew up. Perhaps that was part of the problem. By nature, I was a homebody. I wanted nothing more than to be a wife and mother and the security of a real homestead, and I wanted peace at all cost. I was not a fighter. I was not assertive. I was a quiet, introverted, easy-going person. That was the person I wanted to remain. But life had other ideas. All I asked of life was tranquility. What I got was constant assault on my composure.

During my years of marriage, I recoiled from violent control like a timid creature crouching in the woods, waiting for danger to pass. I somehow got the message that in order to deserve love, I had to be perfect. So whenever things went wrong in the marriage, I searched my conscience for answers to why it was happening. I believed I must somehow be responsible for the confusion.

As a child, I had been fiercely independent. By age ten, I traveled each Sunday on two buses into the city to spend the day at the theater where there was a stage show between movies. No one ever questioned my independence and I thought it perfectly feasible to do whatever interested me. I never feared it might not be safe for a child my age to have such adventures alone. It seemed perfectly natural to take responsibility for myself. So during the early years of marriage, I felt that familiar sense of responsibility, but soon realized that, no matter what I did, it made little difference. I no longer made the decisions for my life.

The phone jolted my thoughts from the past. It was my mother. She called to tell me that she had spoken with her cousin, Polly, who unexpectedly ran into my father. I hadn't heard from my father for nine years. I saw him very seldom during my early years, and even less as an adult. He was usually intoxicated and had little time for family. When I last saw him, my son, Johnny, was four months old. Johnny was in his playpen on the back porch of my home when my father, who had been drinking heavily, attempted to pick him up from the playpen, missed, and fell onto the concrete slab. Thinking of what could have happened to my baby, I asserted myself for the first time with my father and told him to leave and not come back unless he could visit while sober. He left in a huff. The next day he returned, but never got out of his car. I could tell by his careless driving that he had again been drinking, so I didn't go out. He drove off recklessly and never contacted me again.

Polly told my mother that my father, who was recovering from serious stomach surgery, no longer drank and would like to see me. I didn't know what to do. The very year that my marriage ended, my mother moved back from California to live near me. She relocated because she too had started drinking heavily and needed someone to care for her. Was I to have my father's alcoholism to care for as well? I was confused. I wanted to do the right thing, but what was the right thing? Had he really stopped drinking? I had so many problems that I could barely handle already that one more crisis could have pushed me over the edge. I prayed about it. I asked God to guide me. Life constantly presents questions and it's in searching for the answers that we are forced to examine our inner selves. It's amazing what we discover tucked away in those hidden corners.

A few days later, I called my father and welcomed him into my life again for whatever it might hold. Life gives us miracles, big and small. I was about to experience one of those miracles, for my father became the emotional and monetary support we needed to survive. He cosigned and gave me the additional money I needed to get into an apartment. He didn't have a lot of money, but he shared what he had with us. He helped us willingly and was the male influence Joe and Debralee needed. I remembered my prayer during our stay at the convent. "Please, God," I had prayed, "give me a sign so I will know I've done the right thing. Send me the help I need." God does answer prayer.

We were able to help my father as well. The many people he had treated badly during his years of excess drinking had since died. He had no one through whom to redeem himself, except through my children and me. I believe my father experienced more inner growth during those years than in all the other years of his life. It was a mutual period of growth for both of us. We learned to care for each other as father and daughter for the first time and I learned that it's never too late, if we don't give up on each other.

On a clear autumn afternoon, we moved into our own apartment. Of course, we had no furniture. So, once more, the floor became our bed, as well as our table and our dresser drawers. The good thing about it was that it took very little to keep it clean!

Then after four months of living off the floor, a lady at work moved to Florida and sold me twin beds, a dresser, and a living room rug, along with assorted dishes, utensils, pans and odds and ends. My father helped me pay for them. The floor became a memory.

Then I went shopping for living room furniture. At that time, it was not easy for a single woman with no employment track record to get credit on her own. So I found the furniture I wanted, filled out the credit form for Mr. and Mrs. Rooney, and wrote that Mr. Rooney was self-employed. I waited to see if *we* would be approved. The furniture arrived six weeks later. After I had made five payments, I requested that the charge be put in my name only, as Mr. Rooney no longer lived at my address and I would be making the payments. Next month's bill reflected that change.

Then, the first of December I began to think about Christmas. Debralee and Joe had very little clothing and Joe had left all his toys behind that fateful night, except for his stuffed animals. By then I had an old second-hand car my father had bought me for $50.00, so I drove to a department store in a neighboring town where I had once purchased on a 90-day charge.

I took the elevator to the credit office and walked over to the counter. "Good morning," I managed. "I'm here to make some purchases using your 90-day charge."

The woman behind the counter looked at me over her horn-rimmed glasses. "I'm sorry," she said, "we no longer have a 90-day charge, but you can fill out our regular credit application."

My heart sank. Somehow I had to make this work and I knew they would turn me down if they knew my circumstances. "I don't understand. I called just this morning and was told that if I came in, I could use your 90-day charge," I fibbed.

"I'm sorry for the inconvenience. I can't imagine who could have told you that."

"Well...I drove here expecting to shop," I said with a trace of outrage in my voice, my stomach quivering.

"Well … if you'll fill out our application, you will be approved in about four weeks."

"Four weeks? I'm sorry. I had planned to do some shopping today, but if that's not possible, I'll go elsewhere," I said, desperately wondering where that might be.

"Well ... let me see," she said. "If you fill out the application, I suppose I can at least get you started with $300 in merchandise certificates. How would that be?" She reached in the drawer and pulled out the certificates. What beautiful — multicolored party money! *There is a Santa Claus*, I thought, *and she has red hair and horn-rimmed glasses.* I set a record that day for shopping in the least amount of time; afraid they would discover what my Santa had done and cancel the certificates.

Another Christmas gift arrived just before the holidays. Due to my husband's emotional disability, Joe was eligible for Social Security benefits. Right before Christmas, I received my first check. My salary was not quite enough for the rent, food and other necessary expenses, so the social security check was the child support I needed so desperately to help pay our rent each month. "Thank you, God," I said, feeling a deep sense of gratitude.

Even with the blessings that had come our way, Christmas was a sad time for all of us. Debralee tried to pick up Johnny so we could see him over the holidays. It didn't happen and there were no organizations or persons in authority to intercede. I went into a deep inner depression, coupled with heightened anxiety. I tried to hide it from my children but I know they could see it in my eyes. I could see it in my eyes as the mirror reflected my image. It was as if the light had been turned off as the dark clouds of life filled my soul.

#####

When I was very young, Granddaddy had a dog he called Old Henry. I watched him grow from a pup to an aged dog, barely able to get up from his cozy spot by the fire, his limbs seemed so painful. But, in his old age, no matter how much he hurt, Old Henry never missed an opportunity to follow Granddad wherever he went during the day. I never gave it much thought. I figured that's how dogs were. Now, thinking back, I marvel at the bravery of that old black dog. He has become one of my role models. He was faithful to the end. I wondered if I would ever be as brave as Old Henry — or as loving.

Chapter 5 **Life's Many Surprises**

I turned the key in the lock and entered my apartment. All seemed quiet inside. As I entered, I saw that Joe's bedroom door was closed, and heard water running in the bathtub. *Debralee must be taking a shower*, I thought. I went straight to the kitchen. A cup of hot tea would do wonders for me, I considered. I put the kettle on and went back to the living room, easing into a cozy chair. I sat there quietly for a moment, closing my eyes and taking a deep, relaxing breath. Suddenly, Joe came bounding from his bedroom and flopped on the stool at the foot of my chair, his blue eyes sparkling with excitement.

"Well, you look happy," I said through a deep sigh. "What have you been up to?"

"I traded all my old baseball cards today!" he exclaimed.

"And what did you get in return?" I asked

" A *whole bunch* of paper birthday streamers!"

That seemed an odd thing for a six-year-old to trade for his baseball cards. I was curious. "What in the world are you going to do with all those streamers?"

"You like the circus, don't you?" he asked in a fun tone.

"I sure do."

"Do you like surprises?" he asked further.

"Sometimes …" I answered, a bit more cautiously, feeling a slight glimmer of mystical knowledge.

"Well then," he said, "you're gonna love this! Close your eyes and take my hand."

I complied obediently, too tired to do anything else. He led me to his room, then commanded, "Now, don't look till I tell you!" The door snapped open and Joe bellowed, "Open your eyes!"

About the time I blinked my eyes open, the teapot began to whistle at a screaming pitch. In that second of confusion I couldn't distinguish the shriek of the teapot from my own anguished cry.

"Isn't it a beautiful surprise, Mom?"

I thought I would faint! The entire bedroom ceiling was dotted with brightly colored streamers that had been secured with a whole bottle of glue. The streamers hung to the floor, draping casually over the rug like a vivid, cascading waterfall.

I took a deep breath and managed, "I will have to say, Joe, it is beautiful, but it looks like such a ... permanent surprise," and thought about how exhausting it was going to be to scrape the surprise off the ceiling!

Shortly after moving to Greenbelt, I began searching for a lawyer. I had been told that someone in my circumstances could depend on the help of free legal aid. But when I kept my appointment, I was advised to consult with a regular law firm. They said my case was too involved for them to handle. It was a disheartening blow and would push the weeks even farther ahead.

I made an appointment for a consultation with a lawyer from a reputable law firm. After the first meeting, I learned that his retainer fee would be $400, with additional fees as we went forward with the case. That was far beyond anything I could come up with and monthly payments, it seemed, were out of the question. I couldn't afford him on my salary and my father didn't have that kind of money. Months later, through an acquaintance, I met a lawyer who agreed to receive his fee when the case was resolved. He knew there would be a settlement because of the house, although, in those days, the property was only worth $20,000.

It took eighteen months just to get my case into court, and the lawyer did little to fight for my rights. During this time, my husband violently denied me the right to see Johnny. With the hope of an early court date slipping away and the months merging into a year, I began to sink into deep despair. I filled my time with activity and people. I ran from the suffering until I was exhausted. I didn't want to feel the anguish. For years, I had heard again and again that everything happens for a reason. How could such terrible conflict ever be beneficial? It would be years before I quit struggling and allowed the lessons that come from life's small deaths and rebirths to change me.

The divorce trial resembled the "good old boys club." The judge demanded that I comply with my husband's wishes for reconciliation. Again, I was a *possession* who was out of control, all that I had suffered invalidated. The judge wagged his finger at me and yelled, "Do you hear your husband, young woman, he wants a reconciliation."

The only way I could finally convince him that it wasn't going to happen was to be quite blunt and blurt out, "Over my dead body!"

With that, the judge stopped badgering, but made it clear that I wasn't going to gain anything. There would be no divorce at that time and custody of the boys would remain split. In the early `70s, there was a three-year waiting period for a spouse to contest a divorce. My husband took it to the limit, so it was three and a half years before the divorce was granted.

By spring, I decided to ask the sisters at Johnny's parish school if they would arrange a meeting between Johnny and myself. They agreed, and provided an empty office. Just after lunch, Johnny walked into the room, taller than when I saw him last. I searched his face for any sign of emotion. I found none. He stood before me staring idly at the floor.

"Hello, Johnny," I said softly, blinking to hide my tears. "Please come here."

He moved closer, nervously twisting the button on his jacket. I reached out and pulled him on my lap, folding my arms around him. His body became rigid. I could no longer hold back the tears. I wanted to pick him up and run from the school. I might have done just that if Johnny had not been so unresponsive. I didn't know how to handle it and I didn't want to further traumatize him. "How would you like to see your brother?" I asked. He didn't answer — just shrugged his shoulders. He and his little brother had been so close. What had happened to his feelings?

The recess bell penetrated the room. "I have to go now!" John blurted out.

"You can stay longer." I pleaded.

"I can't," he said, as he quickly slid off my lap and bolted for the classroom door. Suddenly, Johnny was gone. I sat there in shocked despair. What had happened to all we had shared for nine years? I was heartbroken. How could that bond simply disappear? I slowly gathered my things and prepared to leave the school grounds. As I walked to my car, I could hear the shrill laughter of children at play. Those happy voices rang in my mind for months until, in the clamor of everyday living, I could no longer hear them.

After twenty-one years of marriage and four beautiful children, I became one of the statistics I had tried so hard to avoid. My mother had been divorced twice and my father four times. I never wanted to be a casualty of divorce and it took years for me to face the reality that ignoring my problems was not the same as solving them

#####

I once read that when Jesus said that we should pray, by

believing that we already have, he was announcing the Law of Cause and Effect. We plant the seed and a natural process will produce a plant like the pattern in the seed. This is how faith operates. The seeds of today are the fruits of tomorrow. All I could do that day was to pray that somehow I had planted the seed of love in Johnny's heart and that the spiritual cause and effect would one day produce from life's natural process a sustaining devotion to one another.

Chapter 6 **Poor Little Princess**

I thought about what had led up to the divorce. The marriage had never been good, but after the birth of my fourth child, my husband began treatment for an emotional disorder that had been building for years. During his treatment he was hospitalized for six months. I attended group therapy sessions six nights a week in the hope of helping him regain his health. Of course, this meant that each evening I had to leave the girls, who were just barely into their teens, to look after the two boys, only two and four years old. Joe, the baby, was usually screaming at the front gate as I pulled away in the car, but the doctors said it was imperative that I attend the meetings, so I did what was needed. As it turned out, those sessions were a turning point in my life.

Looking back, I see where I was ready for personal growth, although at the time I didn't realize it, or was too afraid to recognize it. One evening, the crack in the mold broke, never to be mended again. Humpty Dumpty took on real meaning for me. There were about thirty patients and family members in the meeting with the doctor and a couple of nurses. I was sitting next to a young fellow who had come to the hospital after suffering an emotional breakdown while studying at the local university. The first meeting that I had attended, this young man had been at his worst, screaming and pounding at the door of a padded cell. But now he had improved so much that they were getting him ready to go out into society once again.

I usually kept a low profile, hoping no one would ask me questions and I could simply sit quietly and observe. That evening, however, the doctor decided it was my turn to discuss my problems. He asked why I permitted the things in my marriage that were so oppressive. I folded my hands in my lap ever so demurely. What I wanted to say was that I was scared to death and had never been able to get anyone to really listen to my plight. What I actually said was, "Well, when you marry it's for better or for worse, and if you get the worst, it must be God's will."

The young patient sitting next to me turned, looked squarely at me, and said, "Lady, you must be crazier than I am."

I will forever be grateful to that young man for his comment. But at the time, I was outraged. How dare he intimate that I had a problem? I was simply a victim.

I cried all the way home and well into the night. Things came up from the depths of me that I didn't even know were there — things I had kept carefully buried so as not to cause a disturbance. It was true that I had lived as a victim and didn't see a way out. But something was different now. My perfection had been challenged. The mold had been broken. I asked to see my own counselor.

In the year that followed, I changed so rapidly inside that I had to run to keep up with myself. There had been years of having to filter my thoughts through someone else's mind before I could make a decision or voice an opinion. Now I heard myself say to the counselor, "No, I don't want to live this way any longer." And finally, "No, I *will not* live this way any longer." I realized I had been waiting for the world to give me permission to be myself. The world never did, but during that year I learned to give *myself* permission. From that moment on, I was not the same person as before, and somehow it didn't matter if I was perfect. I wanted to live.

During the probing by the doctors into my personality, I mentioned that I liked writing poetry. They wanted to see a sample. Oddly enough, without even realizing it, I brought in possibly the one poem that was most revealing of how I felt. When they analyzed the poem, they pointed out that, while I had written it from the vantage point of a child, I was, in reality, crying out for someone to notice what was happening to me. I realized the doctors were right.

The poem read:

Poor Little Princess

> When the sandman comes to Betty and Tim and the house is quiet and the lamps are dim, we turn the covers down a bit to romp and play till it's time to quit. Just Panda Bear, and Andy and me, we're as happy and pleased as a dolly can be. But poor little Princess never has any fun, only sits on her chair from sun to sun. She's a beautiful doll, with a satin dress, but she never smiles ... poor little Princess. No one's allowed to take her down. Why she's never even been to town. I remember the Christmas she came to stay. How she loved the ride in Santa's sleigh. Now, she sits all alone in the corner there, watching Betty and Tim with a hollow stare. She'd rather be a rag doll, too, and have some fun, the way we do. So, if ever you see your best doll in distress, remember the sad ... poor little Princess.

For twenty-one years I did as I was told or all of us paid the consequences. I complied most of all so that my children would have as close to a normal life as possible. I also never wanted to start anything I couldn't handle; I didn't know how to make a transition from the life I was living to something better and the times when I took the children and left, there was really no place to go — only temporary shelters in the homes of friends for a day or two until he found us. Now, everything was different. I was different. Even the year before the fateful night I left, I began the process of changing. I was becoming stronger. I had enrolled in night school against my husband's wishes. When he threw out my books, I went without them. When he tore up my papers, I wrote them again. When he no longer allowed me to take the car, I walked the hour it took to get there.

I continued to push and test the parameters. It was as if something inside me was being compelled to change — to change myself, my life, my world. And I felt more confident because our family life wasn't a secret anymore. People in authority were beginning to care. Looking back, I realized that I had become a prisoner of war and a coconspirator in my own misery. It was difficult to regain my personal power. It was a frightening experience to trust in my inner guidance. I had lived a secret life of silent despair and the pain and confusion weighed me down until I no longer felt the inner joy.

#####

Growing up, I had a beloved cat for thirteen years named Bluey. She trusted me and always looked to me for her needs. She had many litters of kittens over the thirteen years of her life, but I recall the year she had three babies in the early spring. We made a bed for them in a cardboard box in the basement.

As the days grew warmer, Bluey would gather her babies in mid-day and, one by one, carry them out to the yard, depositing them in a glass case that my grandmother had fashioned for her new seedlings to give them a good start before planting. I guess Bluey thought this would be an ideal place for her babies, since the glass protected them from the early spring breeze.

I don't know what kept Bluey away most of that afternoon, or if she simply forgot where she had put them. But, as the evening sun was going down, I remember sitting on my bed as Bluey came through the open window carrying one of her kittens. She laid it on the bed and went back twice more for the others.

Perhaps the sun had gotten hotter than usual that day. Maybe the glass had shut out the oxygen the baby kittens needed to breathe. Whatever the cause, all three babies were dead. Bluey kept looking at me, pleading, with constant meows. She wanted me to do something to help her kittens. She believed that I could save them. I wondered if she would ever understand that I didn't have that kind of power.

This was how I felt now. I was searching for someone with enough power to help me live again. It would take awhile before I understood that it was God I was searching for.

Chapter 7 <u>Childhood Memories</u>

My early years were often filled with uncertainty. My parents divorced before my first birthday and my memory of them was, not as a couple, but as two individuals who were connected to each other only through me. Because my mother was having a difficult time adjusting to being a single parent and the demands of a job, I lived with my paternal grandparents until I entered first grade. I saw my parents only on occasion. I can't say those were unhappy years. My grandparents were devoted to me and I to them. My grandfather was my hero and my grandmother a model of quiet strength. Since there were no other children to interact with in the secluded area where they lived, I became the great entertainer. My patient grandmother was my audience and there was a new show everyday. During my formative years, I lived in a world of love and contentment. It was the mid-30s to early 40s, when no one locked their doors at night — where strangers meant one thing — someone was hungry and in need of charitable nurturing.

We had no refrigerators; each kitchen had an icebox. Everyday the iceman delivered a chunk of ice, and neither he nor the milkman ever knocked at the kitchen door; they simply walked in and deposited their wares in the icebox. If someone from the family was home there would be a friendly greeting. If not, they went on to the neighbor's house. It was a simpler time when baseball blared from radio sets during the summers and, on cold winter nights, the family huddled by the fire to listen on the radio to *The Shadow Knows*.

At age six, I moved from my grandparents' home to live with my mother, spending weekends and summers with my grandparents. My mother lived in city dwellings; a very different atmosphere from the country living of my grandparents, but the diversity gave me a strong sense of flexibility. It also helped foster my imagination. Because I was a "city girl" and a "country girl" simultaneously, each environment provided a unique opportunity to explore different sides of my personality — a personality that, during that time, resulted in a vast inner life in the form of fantasies. I was a daydreamer of great scope and adored music and the world of entertainment. Reality held little interest for me — perhaps because my world had already taken on too much "reality."

My mother remarried and, while my stepfather was good to me, he and my mother were not compatible. Violent outbursts became a big part of our lives. I often felt fearful and anxious, never knowing when the outbursts would come. They were both strong individuals with little fear of one another. I was the one who felt the fear from the eruptions and felt I had no one to turn to. I was by nature perceptive and sensitive to the feelings of others, and the strife I experienced forced me even further inside myself. I was an only child until the age of ten when my brother, David, was born. With the age difference, I was more a second mother than a sibling. Even David said later that he remembered me taking care of him more than he recalls Mama. With my mother and step-father's relationship becoming more and more explosive, they divorced shortly after my brother was born.

The memories of my early years are those of self-isolation. What I couldn't cope with, I simply ignored. I went even deeper inside my inner world, finding consolation in a world of my own creation. Looking back, I believe that was the only real control I felt I had over my life.

My mother was a vibrant, fun-loving person. Everyone loved her personality. She had lots of friends and was the life of every party. The downside for me was that I was never invited to the party. Mama was good to me and I always knew she loved me, but she wanted to remain forever young and carefree. I have vivid memories as a first grader of being left alone at night while she went out with friends. I remember covering my head with the blanket when I went to bed so no one could find me. I never blamed her. I seemed to sense her terrible need to pursue happiness at all cost, although I didn't understand it. I sensed that all her life she had yearned for the father who died tragically before she was born. Having no father, my mother's paternal grandfather became her confidant and pal, as mine had.

In her developing years, as in the years that followed, my mother was a rebel, a non-conformist, and always walked a little on the wild side. She was an interesting character and she was absolutely fearless. Perhaps this is the reason I took on such a serious persona as a young person. I was attempting to put some balance in my life. During those years, keeping a balance was as important as it was difficult to maintain.

History seems to repeat in families. My grandfather became my rock. We were inseparable. He took me with him wherever he went and taught me the joys of gardening and the quiet love of nature. He owned a country store that became a meeting place for many of the elderly men around the area. In the center of the store sat an imposing black, potbellied stove and in the evenings the men would sit near the stove to warm themselves and argue politics. I was always in the midst of those debates. I loved it.

When I was fourteen, my grandfather became gravely ill. I was losing my rock. He slowly deteriorated from diabetes. He lost a leg and eventually lost his sight from the disease. He died when I was eighteen. It was during the time of my grandfather's illness that I met the man I would marry. I was desperately trying to recapture that lost strength, but the strength I perceived in my husband, he used for control. He brought a volatile demeanor to the marriage, I brought my timidity. I am not placing blame. He has his journey just as I have mine and I see now, after all these years, that men are also victims of their abusive behavior

#####

I recall, at the age of ten, wanting to be like everyone else, so much so that when the teacher at school went over our nutrition program, I lied. We were to write down what we had for breakfast each morning. I was embarrassed to say that I hadn't eaten at all. There was cereal in the pantry but I didn't like sitting at the table alone in the mornings, so I skipped breakfast. When the teacher read some of the menus to the class, I was glad I had lied. I made up a most nutritional menu and thought, if she reads mine, everyone will think that breakfast for me is family time. I wanted so much to have family time. Now that I'm all grown up, I still long for it.

Chapter 8 **Ms. Rooney, Take A Letter**

Life got more involved. I enrolled in night classes to brush up on basic office skills, including typing. It was the typing that almost kept me from applying for an office job, but as happened in my marriage, life began pulling in opposite directions until I had to finally make a choice.

Early one Monday morning, I drove into D.C. to take a civil service test for a government job. I had nearly completed my evening classes in typing and business. I needed a higher salary and decided it was time I got an office job.

I walked in to find that there were about 150 of us who were there to take the government test and, after taking the written exam, we were herded into a huge room with a sea of typewriters. I had been nervous about taking the typing test, but now, in the midst of all the others, I felt a wonderful anonymity.

The instructor gave us the signal to begin typing. I did as my class teacher at school had instructed, never once taking my eyes off the test material to look at the typewriter. When the test ended, I was certain it went well and was glad to have it behind me. Then I looked at my test paper for the first time. To my horror, there was nothing on the paper. It seemed that the person before me had put the typewriter on stencil. With 150 of us in the room, my typewriter was the only one on stencil. I asked to take the test again, but was told I would have to wait six months to retake it. It was discouraging. Six months seemed an eternity and I wanted out of my job.

Then I heard of a similar test being given in Virginia for the Navy Department. I made a call and was scheduled for the following week. When I arrived that day I discovered it was quite a different set up. There were only eight of us and during the test the instructor walked around the tiny room looking over our shoulders, commanding, “Keep those fingers on the keys ... you need to pass this test the first time!” The instructor stopped to look over my shoulder more than once. I became totally intimidated. My hands began to tremble so badly that I could no longer keep them on the proper keys. It was a terrible experience and I failed miserably. My self-confidence plummeted to an all-new low.

Having heard of my two experiences, my typing instructor at school said she would administer the typing test during class. I was relieved. Somehow I envisioned the class as a whole taking the test, but when I arrived, I found I was the star of the evening. I discovered that my desk and typewriter were situated so that I faced the class. This was bad enough, but then we realized that an adapter was needed for the electrical outlet into which the typewriter had to be plugged, so my instructor borrowed one from another class. That class instructor said he wouldn’t need it until the second half of the class, but as I began my typing test, I was aware of the man standing outside the classroom door, peering in through the small glass window, waiting for his adapter.

At the instructor’s prompt, I began to type. I suddenly felt like a freak in a sideshow. Everyone was looking at me and at the end of each of the three tests she had me type, they gave a unanimous sigh and asked, “How did you do?” How did I do? It was one of the most horrendous episodes I had ever been through. Everyone in the class meant well, as did the instructor — they were truly concerned for me, but I have never been so nervous or so humiliated in my life. It was a huge disaster!

My divorce hearing was finally scheduled. This time there was a different judge who was very sympathetic that the two boys had been separated from each other for so long, with visitation rights not being honored. As usual, my husband told the judge that we couldn’t divorce. The judge asked him why. He said he had slept with me. So the judge asked him where he had slept with me. He told him it was down at the Greenbelt Lake.

Then it was my turn to take the stand. The judge asked me if I had slept with Mr. Rooney. I told him, "Judge, if I can't do better than the Greenbelt Lake, forget it."

The divorce was made final and the judge said he was going to look into why the boys had been separated for so long and it would be resolved. I waited for a month for word from the judge. When I heard nothing, I called the courthouse. I was told the judge had retired. It seemed that everywhere I turned, there was a dead-end.

My job was getting more and more difficult. I began to realize that a woman who had a husband at home was treated differently from a woman who did not. If there was a problem and a husband intervened, treatment by management was much more affable. I witnessed this on a few occasions when my coworkers' husbands came in to confront a situation. Management quickly backed down.

I was one of the select few at the store who was given a job referred to as "putting up bread." This meant coming in before the store opened to fill the shelves in the bakery with bread and baked goods. Sounds simple, but in order to accomplish this I had to work with stacks of trays that towered three feet over my head. To reach the top tray, I had to stand on the edge of the bottom tray, reach up over my head, and swing the trays onto the floor. They were heavy and awkward. It was a terrible treatment of a women's body, but in my case, it was even more harmful. I had been diagnosed with uterine fibroid tumors and was waiting for my doctor to determine if surgery was my only option. Lifting was clearly harmful. It was difficult enough to stand all day and lift the groceries into the carts, but my doctor warned me to stop the additional heavy lifting.

I approached management and explained the situation, not

doubting for a minute that they would object. I thought it was taken care of, especially since there were only a few of us given that job and plenty of others to assign. But to my astonishment, when the next work schedule was posted, I was again scheduled to "put up bread." When I protested and said I would bring in a statement from my doctor, I was told that if I did this, I would be out of a job because that would show I was incapable of doing the work.

I've read that life continues to give us similar circumstances until we face our fears and learn the lessons life wants to teach us. I believe, in my case, life had a real struggle. I knew the lesson I needed to learn most was assertiveness, to stand up for myself, but it seemed to require more grit than I had among my natural resources, and I was always afraid of the consequences. However, both my parents were fighters who never let anyone get the best of them. Somewhere inside me, I considered, surely there was a small "chip off the old block." With life continually forcing me to fight for myself, I was beginning to discover that there was. That week I exchanged the "bread day" with another employee for her regular day. Later, I was told by management that I could not exchange my day with anyone again, and that the other employee would be penalized if I did so.

The next week, I was given another day to stack bread. I told management, "I can't do it. I will give the day away to someone else and lose a day's pay — something I can't afford."

"You can't do that. You have to work your schedule," I was told. "And you don't want another employee to be penalized, do you?"

"Then you can mark me ill that day, because I won't be in."

"You do that," management said, "and you won't have a job when you come back. You women are all alike. We're doing you a favor lettin' you work here. Who else would hire you?"

The next week I stayed home the day I was scheduled to stack bread. The next workday, I found I had not lost my job. However, the following week, the work schedule reflected three bread days. I was told I could not switch with anyone nor could I give my days away. I was required to work my schedule as posted.

Not long after that I had my surgery, and management said that when I returned to work I would again be given the job of stacking bread, although my doctor strongly advised against it. I couldn't understand this treatment. It was as if the men who ran management had a grudge against women and had found someone unprotected and vulnerable enough for them to vent their anger. They liked bullying and I was indeed vulnerable. They knew I couldn't afford to be out of a job.

I began to pray in earnest that God would intervene. The thought of a typing test kept me from applying for an office job, but I knew I couldn't persevere much longer under those tyrannical circumstances. How on earth had I finally left an oppressive marriage only to find the same treatment on a job?

Reading the want ads made matters worse. I felt so unqualified reading the glowing description of the person who should apply for the job. Then I heard from a friend that there was a job opening at the local university. She gave me the supervisor's telephone number and I phoned during my lunch break. The job was for an off-campus coordinator, working in the university's bookstore. My one concern was "would there be a typing test?" When I was told there wouldn't, I heard little else. I wanted that job, and surprisingly, they wanted me. What I hadn't stopped to consider was that they hired me over the phone, sight unseen, and with no references. It didn't matter.

I took great pleasure in presenting my resignation.

"What's this?" Gene asked when I handed him the envelope.

"I'm resigning," I said, trying to keep my broad smile from

illuminating the entire store.

"You're resigning? What's the job?" he sneered.

"I'm the new Off-Campus Coordinator for the University." I could see he was impressed. I was pretty impressed myself. However, that feeling of euphoria would soon be mixed with anxiety, as stark reality set in.

#####

When I was eleven, I would take a bus and then a streetcar and go alone to Glen Echo, a huge amusement park many miles from home. My big thrill in those days was to see how many times I could ride the roller coaster before my money ran out. I would ride it over and over until it took my breath away. I felt so brave, as if I could endure anything that came my way. Now I have many things to endure but I don't feel so brave. Do children have a built-in sense of God's protection? What happens to that feeling as we grow older? I miss that brave little girl.

Chapter 9 **On The Job Training**

I was exhilarated the day I began my new job. I love books, so I felt that working in a bookstore was going to be very exciting. I didn't know how exciting! Actually, it was a good experience. It brought out abilities I wasn't aware of and brought them out instantaneously. In fact, the very first day, out of necessity, I discovered that I could think fast and move just as quickly. It felt good to realize this about myself after so many years of low self-esteem.

My supervisor was a woman who was low-keyed but quietly forceful. Evette knew the job well. It had been her job before being promoted to supervisor of the textbook office. She was an interesting character who was perpetually trying to quit smoking. From the day I met her until I left the job, she was stuck on the same numbered filter in a series of filters guaranteed to stop the smoking habit. She became my stability and I listened intently to everything she said. I had to. In fact, the moment I arrived on the job, she told me not to take off my coat because we were going "off campus" — whatever that meant.

We immediately got into a big white panel truck containing lots of books and related materials. We were going to the Pentagon, she alerted. On the way, I was told what I would be expected to do once we got there, and I was to pay attention, she said, "because tomorrow you will go by yourself to another location and supervise three guys." I would what? Today I will learn this aspect of my job and tomorrow I'll supervise three men? How could this be? But there was no time to wonder about it, so I paid close attention to every word she said. When the truck rattled so loudly I couldn't hear what she was saying, I read her lips. The thought occurred to me as the panel truck jostled in and out of potholes that maybe no one had wanted this job, especially the in-house people who knew what to expect. However, I didn't have time to dwell on it. I had to absorb all of Evette's instructions as we were approaching the Pentagon.

When we arrived, I discovered that we were setting up a temporary bookstore to sell materials to students who did not actually attend classes at the university, but who were taking accredited courses. A cash register was put in place and, as people gathered, I had to quickly find the materials they needed, write up receipts, ring the sales on the cash register, and replenish the tables. I had to work quickly, as there was a time limit for the students who had to return to their jobs.

What made the job so difficult was that, while I was out of the office for those weeks selling the materials, I was also expected to accomplish the second part of my job, which was to order both nationally and internationally the books and course materials for Open University classes. All this had to be done in a timely manner before the students began coming in or calling for the books they needed. But that seemed insignificant to what I experienced when the material began arriving at the bookstore. When the boxes arrived, I had to run from the back room with heavy boxes of books, tear the boxes open, and coordinate the books with additional material from other boxes to make complete sets for each of the Off-Campus courses (and the boxes gave no clue as to which course materials they contained).

Two tables were set up in the aisle of the bookstore for me. The problem was that university students were searching in that aisle for books as well. When a student needed to look on the shelves, I had to take time out until I could use the space again. During this time, the phones in the office were ringing from students asking when they could pick up their materials. Of course, they could only pick them up once I had time to put the sets together. So I worked from 60 to 70 hours a week during the fall book rush to get the job done, and there was no overtime pay. I did what I had to do. It was my job and somehow I was going to have that course material ready when the students needed it — and I did. The store manager had told me that there would be an increase in salary when the book rush was over because of my extra efforts, so I worked even harder to earn that increase, but my realization of why the in-house employees hadn't wanted the job was becoming crystal clear.

Just before the spring rush, Evette stunned me by saying I needed to go to Personnel for a typing test. "Why?" I asked. "I'm doing the job, which includes light typing. Why do I need a typing test?" She said it was needed for my records. So there I was on my way to Personnel, asking God once again for help. I had to pass that test.

I was extremely nervous. Thankfully, the woman giving the test put me in a room by myself. Then she set a timer and left the room, leaving the door slightly ajar. "Dear, God," I prayed, "I don't know how you're going to do it, but I really have to pass this typing test." In order to filter out the noises from the outer office and concentrate, I focused on the test and heard nothing from that point on until the lady reentered the room again. I honestly did not hear the timer go off. The next thing I knew, she was standing over me saying, "Oh dear, I didn't hear the timer. Oh, well," she said with a shrug, "I suppose it doesn't matter." It mattered to me. I barely passed the test. Without that additional time, I am certain I would have failed. "Thank you, Lord," I whispered.

During the spring rush, I worked as hard as I had during the fall rush. I finally asked the store manager about my raise since it hadn't been mentioned again. He told me he had never made that promise. I felt devalued. It really hurt. But I was learning that I had options. I didn't have to remain in circumstances where I was not appreciated. It was okay to choose something else for myself.

Weeks later, I heard about a job opening in the Dean's Office at one of the university libraries. I applied. When I interviewed for the job I made it quite clear that if they were looking for a typist, I was not the person for the job. The man who hired me said he had been looking for three months for the right person, I was that person, and no, it was not a job for a typist. So I went to work in the Dean's Office.

My first day on the new job I was terribly intimidated to learn that my boss was a spectacular typist. In fact, he typed 90 words a minute. I had somehow developed a real phobia about typing. But, what was that to me? I had already told them I was not a typist.

My desk was situated in the middle of a small room. My boss, whose desk faced mine, was no more than ten feet away. On the other side of my desk, about three feet from me, sat a man whose job it was to listen for the phone. Once it rang, he bolted for the door to do whatever it was he did. It was never clear to me exactly what his job was. Most of his time, however, was spent sitting sideways in his chair looking bored and staring at me. To make matters worse, they gave me pages of computer language materials and told me to type them. I was to type them? It had to be a joke! It was no joke. I was terrified. Not only did I have to type with an audience staring at me, but I had to type in a technical language I didn't understand. It was so quiet in the office that when I attempted to use the typewriter, all that could be heard was the sound of my typing, and I did not type 90 words a minute. I turned to God in desperation. "Lord, I am trusting you with all my heart to do something. Just get me started. I am absolutely frozen with fear. If I don't produce soon, I will lose this job and I can't go back to the bookstore. Please, just get me started. I'll take care of the rest." I whispered.

Within five minutes of my prayer, I heard a terrible racket

outside my window. They were tearing up the sidewalk with jackhammers. It was so loud that my boss and the "phone guy" moved into another office and not one person could hear me typing over the racket outside. It was wonderful. All I could say was — "Thank you, Jesus!"

I was only on that job a short while when I was offered a new position, working for someone I knew who had started his own company and wanted me as the office manager. He offered me a higher salary than I was making and the job seemed to have great potential. I thought it was a dream come true. I had already decided, in spite of my fears, that I would say "yes" to life. I would simply step out on faith wherever God would lead me. I had no idea what an office manager did, but I would learn, even if I had to teach myself. So I left the university for still another job that seemed to hold such promise, and began to build another *ant hill.*

#####

Many animals have the kind of devotion that we humans can't always grasp. When I was about four years old and living with my grandparents, my mother gave me two baby ducklings for Easter. One of them died, but the other lived and grew into quite a large and handsome duck. Being at the cartoon-loving age, I named my duck, Donald. He was an adoring playmate and followed me wherever I went, happily quacking at my heels in duck language as he walked behind my every step.

One afternoon, my grandmother and I went to the movie theater nearly eight blocks from our home. I had made sure the gate was locked so Donald could not get out of the yard. But he was a determined friend. We had just purchased our tickets and were about to enter the theater when we heard, "Quack, quack, quack." There was Donald! He had jumped the fence and followed us, somehow sensing the direction we had walked. For years, I marveled at that duck's fondness for me and his determination to follow his dream. I guess I'm a lot like that duck, forever trying to follow my dream. I only hoped I had the same tenacity.

Chapter 10 **The Tap Root**

As a child, I knew very little about God, but I sensed there was something higher than myself. I was instinctively aware that the world must have been created by a power more expansive than anything I had seen, although I knew very little in a religious sense. My family did not attend church, though my grandmother was a very spiritual person. However, when my grandparents went home to Virginia for visits, they attended the small Christian church in their hometown, as they had in their youth.

My first memory of God in a religious context came when my mother and I visited my maternal grandmother in Virginia. While there, my aunt attended Bible classes and I went along. It was my first introduction to a man called Jesus. I recall staring at his picture in a book that the class was following. Somehow that picture, and the words the teacher used to describe him, touched that inner place where I lived, and I felt a spiritual awakening.

At age eleven, I decided that I wanted to become a member of a church. I started out one Sunday morning, planning to enter the very first church I came to. It happened to be an Episcopal Church. I became a member and at age twelve asked to be baptized. I joined the choir and attended Bible classes. It gave my life a sense of order. It also fulfilled a deep need to connect with something spiritual, but it would be a few years before that spirituality became a revealing part of me.

It was during my employment with the university that I experienced for the first time what I call "tapping into my Source." I realized that God had been guiding me and answering my prayers. I had no doubt about this. But this new experience gave me a sense of wonder. Some people might call such an experience a coincidence and that's their prerogative, but for me it was a source of strength.

I had heard of Catholics making something called a novena but, not being raised Catholic, I didn't understand novenas, though I converted to Catholicism in my late twenties. One particular day, a good friend and I visited a priest who was living in a Carmelite Monastery hermitage for the summer months. When we left that day, he picked up a small brochure and handed it to me, asking me to read it when I got home. A few days later, I found the brochure among some papers on my desk and was about to throw it out when I remembered I had told the priest I would read it. I read it with fascination. The brochure contained information about a saint, Saint Therese of the Child Jesus, who avowed, "I will spend my heaven doing good upon earth." The novena was started in 1925 by Father Putigan, a Jesuit priest. During the novena, the priest asked to be presented with a rose as a sign that his prayer was heard and that he would receive an answer. He got his rose more than once and spent his life spreading the novena.

This particular novena is usually said from the ninth to the seventeenth of the month. I glanced at my calendar and realized it was the eighth of the month. That's when I decided I would pray the novena. For the next nine days I prayed and waited to receive my rose. I told only a few people about the novena. One of them was a woman who rode to work with me everyday. She kept asking if I had received my rose. "No," I told her, "but before the end of the novena, I will."

On the last day of my novena, I parked in my usual spot under a tree on the university lot. As I opened the car door, something told me to look at my feet. I looked down at the cement and saw a red rose between my feet. I picked it up, ecstatic over my find! My coworker was speechless. I knew I didn't need a rose for my prayers to be answered, but it was a time in my life when I needed many signs from God because of my insecurities and fears.

I received additional roses at other times while making this novena. One incident that stands out in my mind was while working as office manager. I arrived at my building early one morning and walked down the long hallway to my office. I took off my coat and prepared to start my day. It was mid-January and the possibility of getting a rose seemed remote. I was sitting at my desk when I became aware of a man standing over me holding a red rose. He said he was from another office, although I had never seen him before. He told me he had been to a flower show in Ocean City, Maryland, over the weekend and had brought some roses back with him to the office. "I had forgotten about the flowers," he said, "but when you walked passed my office this morning, something told me that you would like to have one of my roses." A chill went through me. I graciously accepted my rose but didn't tell him about my novena. I felt very blessed.

There is a postscript to my novena experiences. I think I was getting to be too much for Saint Therese to handle alone. After all, I was becoming more and more self-determined. This particular time, I made the novena and waited for my rose. It never came. Then, toward the last day of the novena, I went out to my car and on the ground, right by the door on the driver's side, lay a marigold. What happened to my rose? I was so curious that I picked up the marigold and went back into my apartment to look up "marigold" in the dictionary. To my surprise, one of the definitions listed under marigold was "Mary, Mother of Jesus." I couldn't help laughing. Was Saint Therese telling me to take my problems to the Virgin Mary? "Okay, Therese," I said, "I can take a hint. I guess it's time I got to know her more intimately."

Shortly after starting the novenas, I read the book about St. Theresa's life. I waited until I went to bed one evening to start the book. Once I was settled in my bed, I opened the book and, to my shocked surprise, the entire room filled with the scent of roses. It only lasted a few seconds, but the next day I asked a nun who was a good friend and was versed in the knowledge of the novenas. She calmly told me that the scent of roses is a phenomenon that sometimes happens when starting St. Theresa's book. I felt blessed.

There were many changes taking place in my life at that time. It doesn't take a lot of living to realize that change in life is inevitable. But change can be threatening. Change can foster feelings of doubt and fear — the very things we are told in the Bible to renounce. Doubt and fear are deadly emotions and cling to the psyche like parasites. Napoleon Hill wrote in his book, *You Can Work Your Own Miracles*: "Change is the device by which the eternal verities of life, the habits and thoughts of people, are continuously reshaping themselves into a better system of human relations leading toward harmony and better understanding..." He further said, "The fears and the failures of people, the shocks and disappointments in human relations, are all designed to shake us loose from habits to which we so tenaciously cling."

I believe that my doubts and fears were so great that life took over in answer to my prayer, "God, lead me" — and began to "loose me from the habits to which I so tenaciously clung." Change came often to topple my world and sometimes about all I could do was hold on and trust. I realized that we humans need to constantly fortify and strengthen our sensitive natures. I did a lot of praying. I also began to consume self-help books. I was determined to learn from other people's life experiences and I was inspired and encouraged by their wise counsel. Change can be painful. It's the end of familiarity. Change can make us angry and often anger comes from feelings of fear, the fear that we are losing control. But change is designed to move us to the next stage of development.

During those times of job transitions, several other changes occurred. Kathy married and I became a grandmother at 37 when little Jessica was born. Then Debralee began to date a young man who, after a time, began to show signs of deep emotional problems. Even after she stopped seeing him, he aggressively pursued and harassed her, going so far as to throw himself through the glass balcony door off my living room when she refused to open the front door. This was just one more difficult situation for her to deal with in her young life. She was already struggling with a low self-image and I was concerned about where she was headed in life. She seldom said anything decisive, so on the day she told me she had decided to move to Los Angeles, I nearly died. She could barely take care of herself as it was. How would she survive 3,000 miles away where she knew no one? But it was the way she presented her quest that gave me some confidence that this was indeed something she had to do. She was emphatic about her future for the first time and I felt that if I dissuaded her from going, it would impact her whole life. It was a gut feeling — but I was beginning to trust my intuitive senses.

The day I put her on the plane, I grappled with many emotions. I felt unsettled. I felt fearful for her, but at the same time, there was a certain excitement over the possibilities for her future. I asked God to look after her and to guide her toward a better life. My instincts proved to be beneficial.

When Debralee arrived in Los Angeles, the brother of Kathy's husband, who was in California on vacation, met her at the airport and was to simply drive her through the area until she decided a particular place was right for her. Then he would continue his trip back east.

In the town of Northridge, one of the more exclusive sections of Los Angeles, he stopped to get something out of his trunk. When he did, he accidentally locked the car keys in the trunk of his car. A lady, who had noticed their dilemma, walked out from her yard to ask if she could help. She called a locksmith and, while he was opening the trunk, she talked with Debralee about why she was in Los Angeles. The woman was the wife of the Vice President of the Union Trust Bank and the family welcomed Debralee into their home for the next six weeks. This wonderful lady told me when I met her a few years later that she would like to believe, if it was one of her daughters, someone would do the same. The family helped Debralee to get a car and rent a small house, and most importantly, gave her the time she needed to find a decent job.

One of the few jobs Debralee had before leaving for California was putting components in the back of transistor radios. So this was the type of job she got with a large corporation. But she soon discovered, by a twist of fate, that she had a propensity toward electrical wiring. Through this flair, she was able to create her own job with the corporation and began to market their radar system through the use of computers and presentations. She eventually met her husband, David, who worked for the same company. Going to California changed the entire course of her life. Everything she touched seemed to "turn to gold." It affirmed in me once more Napoleon Hill's advice that, "every adversity has within it the seed of an equivalent benefit." If we explore the possibilities with courage and open our hearts, life will begin to reveal its secrets.

#####

My first day at Kindergarten I became acutely aware of my sense of fair play. My aunt walked me to school that day and when we arrived, I was happy to be there, especially when I saw all the other children. It was short-lived, however, when my aunt told me she was leaving and would come for me when the school day ended. I was upset. I hadn't known she intended to leave me there. That old feeling of abandonment came over me, along with another feeling that I would only understand later on — no one had prepared me for this moment of departure. Everyone had assumed that I would simply accept it and go on with my day. But I couldn't.

I remember retreating to a small playhouse that was erected in the classroom. It looked like a miniature house with windows and a door. I went into the house and closed the door, refusing to come out until my aunt returned for me that afternoon. No amount of coaxing could talk me out of my imposed prison. When my aunt came for me, I asked her if I needed to come back the next day. She said I did, but I was okay with that, because I knew what to expect.

Now my entire family was being tossed about, trying to find where we belonged, and I asked the Lord to prepare us for what was ahead so we could accept it with trust.

Chapter 11 **A Place Called Home**

By this time I had become a solid member of my church and community, and felt I really belonged. All my life I had longed to settle down in a small community where I could walk to neighborhood stores and where the townspeople would know me by name. As a child, I had been uprooted so many times. Even during the years of my marriage, there was little sense of community. The school was at a distance, shopping required a car, and the neighborhood church was not in my neighborhood.

I had no idea what to expect regarding this place called Greenbelt. When my mother came east after years of living in California, she searched the newspapers for a place to settle. She primarily wanted a location where everything was within walking distance, since she didn't drive, and a place she could afford on her limited income. I drove her to many locations and at the end of her search, she decided on Greenbelt. I didn't know it at the time, but I was about to discover the community I had always longed for. For me, Greenbelt held the promise of a better future.

The original City of Greenbelt was an experimental model community. Many of the pioneer residents were Government workers who were looking for a community favorable to family security. The city was built with children in mind and there were many playgrounds with an access through underpasses for traffic safety. The City of Greenbelt has expanded since I first discovered it in 1970, but it is still a great place to live and to raise children.

When we moved to Greenbelt, I enrolled Joe in the parochial elementary school. Joe was only six and starting first grade. Debralee enrolled in the high school a short distance away. I began to work two nights a week with emotionally disturbed children on the request of my former counselor. I did this for a year and a half. It was a wonderful experience. I also helped to establish the first religious classes at my church for children with special needs. In the beginning, I provided the music but, after the first year, I created and conducted the classes. I had never done anything like that before and prayed each week for the Holy Spirit to help me write a lesson plan that would give the children a sense of God's wonder, and every Sunday morning it fell into place. Actually, it was the children who gave me a sense of God's wonder through their loving trust and their appreciation of the little things that bring joy. I used music often in class. Music is a great communicator and children have a natural love for music.

During the most critical years of my marriage, a neighbor gave me an old guitar, and whenever things were the most turbulent, I would play the guitar and write music. Creativity is wonderful therapy. Anything one can do to tap into the depths of the soul helps to ease the suffering. The wonder of creativity is that when we open ourselves to our creative forces, we grow in awareness of who we are and what we are capable of accomplishing.

I took a few guitar lessons offered at one of the public schools. Armed with my new knowledge, I began to compose songs out of my pain and suffering and discovered that music is most therapeutic. In fact, in the midst of the most confusing and debilitating times I would pick up the guitar and compose a song that spoke to my heart. It helped me to heal. It was a way of allowing God to work through me to alleviate my anger and my fears. After I had written what I felt God placed inside me, I felt cleansed. I have continued to use music in this way.

I remember playing one of my songs at a Christmas party given for adults who were suffering from emotional problems. A young man stood in the back of the room during the entire evening. I was told that he never communicated with anyone, never expressed his feelings. After I sang, he walked over to me and said, "What you sang, that's how I feel, but I can't tell anyone.

Thank you."

The song was titled: A Whole Lot of Feeling ~~

Sitting here alone as I watch the evening sky, wondering will tomorrow bring joy or sorrow and asking, Lord, to know the reason why.

For I've got a whole lot of feeling inside, and I wonder if there's anyone to care. What good is the feeling if you have never tried reaching out and giving all you have to share.

Everywhere I go — in the faces that I see, I can find my dreams, all my hopes and schemes, 'cause they're people and they think a lot like me.

For I've got a whole lot of feeling inside, and I wonder if there's anyone to care. What good is the feeling if you have never tried reaching out and giving all you have to share.

Sometimes late at night, when I tell God how I feel, and he sits with me, talking silently, then I know that what I'm longing for is real.

For I've got a whole lot of feeling inside, and I want to give you all I have to share.

When we look for a creative way of expression — no matter what form it takes — God will use it to heal us, and through us, to touch others.

Being part of the Greenbelt community gave me a sense of belonging, and we became members of the local Catholic Church. It was there that I met and became part of a life-long group of friends who helped to affirm in me a sense of self-worth. At the time, I thought this group of women had been friends long before I moved to Greenbelt. I found out later that they had only known each other slightly, and it wasn't until the year I became a member of the church that our relationships began to form. St. Hugh's Church became a magnet for our close circle of friends and we had a wonderful pastor who had a way of drawing the parishioners into the center of the life of Christ. He helped us to develop our special gifts and, through our Bible studies, our friendships with each other deepened. We were all either approaching or had recently reached our fortieth birthday. One's fortieth birthday is quite often a turning point and a time of deep reflection. We had reached a pivotal stage in our lives. We were caught up in a rare and self-actualizing time of joy together — Ann, Lee, Maryliss, Helen, Mary, Ann, Marie, and myself. It was a magic carpet ride. We had found our "Camelot."

At nine, Joe reached a point, much sooner than most, when he decided that going to church was not really doing him any good. So he said he was quitting. I tried to keep calm and gently prodded him each Sunday until I won. But as time went by, it became more difficult to coax him. I would say to God, "I've had it. You do something with him." Just about the time I had exhausted all the ways of getting him interested, I got a call to sing for a home Mass. Joe, of course, did not want to go. We finally compromised. He would go if I let him wear his tennis shoes.

On the way home from Mass that night, Joe said, "I guess I'll have to go see one of the priests tomorrow."

"Why is that, Joe?"

"Well, I'll need to talk to someone if I'm going to be an altar boy."

I almost drove off the side of the road. When I said to God, "do something with him," his response was remarkable.

However, the first Sunday morning that Joe was to serve at Mass as an altar boy he suddenly became fearful. "I can't do it," he moaned. "I just can't go."

"What do you mean, you can't go? You've been to all the classes and you've made a commitment. The priests are depending on you for help."

Joe threw himself across the bed and sobbed. I looked at the clock and realized we had fifteen minutes to get to Mass. I prayed, "God, you got him into this, so you'll have to do something about it and quickly." Finally, Joe agreed, when I convinced him there would be another, more experienced altar boy, to assist him, and that the priest would certainly do everything he could to help. But when we arrived we discovered the other altar boy was ill. Mass was about to begin and there was no time to get a substitute. I told the priest how Joe was feeling and he talked to him to help ease some of his stress.

Joe was so scared that he followed on the heels of the priest as if he was his shadow. There was barely an inch between them wherever they moved. Then it was Joe's turn to walk up the few steps to the altar carrying the glass cruets containing the water and wine.

I had a funny feeling. The long cassock Joe wore over his clothes was a little large. I sat there praying that he wouldn't trip over it. He started up the steps with the cruets on the tray when suddenly it happened. Joe's shoe got caught in the robe and he fell forward up the steps. The congregation let out a muffled cry in unison. I wanted to crawl under the pew and hide. By the grace of God and his angels, Joe held the tray high above his head. Although he had fallen up the steps, the tray and cruets were still intact. He had saved the day! But that wasn't all. When he realized what a heroic act he had performed, he recovered, turned to the congregation and took a low bow. The next thing I heard was applause. I had never seen anything like it in church before. When Mass was over, people came up to shake Joe's hand and tell him what a great job he had done. Joe has always been able to capture an audience.

These were also the terrible years of my court battles and the loss of my son, Johnny. These were transitional years, and without my friends and my church, I am not sure I could have gotten through it. It was during this time that many changes took place in me as a person. This was different from those first few years when I ran from my feelings, filling my life with many activities, never daring to stop my active life for fear of being forced to think. I was scared to think too deeply, even about Johnny. I could have easily fallen into that deep pit of despair and I was afraid I might never find my way out.

Now I was experiencing real growth — such rapid growth that I could hardly keep up with myself. Growth was exciting, but I frequently had to re-evaluate who I was. There seems to be a fine line between learning to curb inner fears and shutting down on emotions. I was learning that when assertiveness is motivated by feelings of fear, it becomes defensive, but coming from a sense of self-actualization, it uses the emotions in a sensitive, practical way to solve problems. Even my signature had changed. Where before it had been small and unassuming, it was now much more notable with flourishes and distinctively creative.

#####

Moving so much as a child, I remember feeling invisible when I'd go in search of other children. Because I was always the "new kid on the block," the children often ignored me. Then, one evening I discovered that if I got their attention long enough to tell a story I invented, I had a captive audience. This became my sense of personal power. It was wonderful. I guess I've been telling stories and vying for attention ever since.

Chapter 12 **Shifting Times**

My first year as office manager was productive and interesting. I had much to learn, but it came together quickly and I felt good about my progress. The second year did not prove so promising. To this day, I am not sure exactly what happened. It seemed to fall apart right before my eyes.

There were only the three of us in the company, me and the two partners, William and Susan. Then later, toward the end of the first year, they hired a part-time bookkeeper to help with the books as the volume of work increased. I guess I was still pretty naive. I honestly didn't realize anything had changed. I knew Susan was not the friendly person she seemed that first year. But I also knew she had gone through a bitter divorce and, because of this, was in counseling for assertiveness training. I tried to keep this in mind and not take her mood swings personally.

At times, it seemed the counseling was changing her rapidly and I was becoming the target of that change. The first year, Susan confided in me about everything that went on in her life. Maybe that was part of the problem. When we moved into larger offices and created a bit more status for ourselves as a company, perhaps I simply knew more as an employee than was comfortable. I was even to stop calling them by their first names — they were now Mr. and Ms. Whatever happened, I began to feel uneasy and insecure in my job. There were too many times when things were blown out of proportion; times when I felt set up and knocked down and wondered — as I did so often in my marriage — what I had done to cause it. My old insecurities emerged and I was terrified of losing my job. I began doubting myself again. I should have confronted the situation, but instead, I allowed it to manifest and create itself while I went into denial. I had hoped things would get better — somehow. That was the vague direction I took. It's never easy to know whether to wait out a situation or to push the parameters. Nothing was clear, no ultimatums given, and I was afraid to ask too many questions. It wasn't until people began phoning the office in answer to an ad placed for my job that I realized my position in the company was actually in jeopardy. At that point, I knew I had better look for something else, but what?

This was a terrible time. My confidence took a backward flip. I remembered the words of the assistant manager at the food chain — "who would hire you?" And I began to sink into those old, out of control, feelings. But I kept thinking that before I was actually out of a job, something good would happen. Many times in my life God has created another avenue when I've needed it, but not this time.

I began interviewing for jobs, but without success. I decided that I would not try another office job. Instead, I would go to bartending school. Bartenders made good money and it would give me time to decide what I really wanted. I prayed about it and God answered, but I wasn't listening.

The day I decided to sign up for bartender's school, I was unable to find the building, so I stopped a stranger on the street to asked for directions. He said to me, "It's right around the corner, but you don't want to do that."

"I don't?" I queried.

"No," he answered, "I've been a bartender for thirty years and, believe me, it's not for you. Find yourself another kind of job."

Why didn't I see that God had sent this stranger my way to deter me? But in my mind I reasoned that if I could just focus on a brand new opportunity, everything would come together. I was wrong.

One day Susan informed me, without saying I was fired, that they were starting a new office manager in two weeks. That was my official notice. That's when it became a reality. The other partner never discussed any of this with me. It was always Susan. She would talk to me about what he had supposedly said, but I never heard it from him. My last day on the job, I left amicably, but inside, I was angry and terrified of the future. That night, at an all time low, I wrote in my journal:

I lie very still...waiting...resigned now that I will not sleep.
For sleep is the attainment of a soul at peace and
not one shouting in the night for tears that will not come.
Oh God, I cannot pray anymore for peace of mind,
but only that the light of morning shall take pity on me
and come early to wake the world,
for in the darkness of my room, I cannot find you this time.

I applied for unemployment benefits. At least that would give us food money and something toward the rent until I got another job. But before receiving my first check, I was notified to come to the unemployment office for a hearing. I didn't understand what was wrong, but kept the appointment.

I soon discovered that my unemployment benefits had been blocked. The mediator at the unemployment office had received the information that I had not been fired, but had quit my job. The mediator could only decide on the facts as they were presented, so it was decided that I would keep my benefits, but would be penalized by forfeiting my first four checks. I still lost. It was five weeks before I received anything and it was three months before I had another full-time job. By now, my father had retired and could no longer help me financially. It was one of the lowest ebbs of my life. I survived through the benevolence of others, for which I will always be grateful, and by working a few temp jobs — offering customers in a grocery store containers of yogurt, and handing out questionnaires to people in cars who stopped for gas at a gas station. Of course, whatever money I earned reduced what I would eventually receive from unemployment. At one point I was fortunate enough to receive a refund check for $20.00 for car insurance I had overpaid. What a godsend!

After completing bartending school, I had two jobs; neither job paid enough to live on. It took only two attempts at bartending to realize the stranger on the street had been right. I was not cut out to be a bartender.

The nation was dealing with the radioactivity scare of Three Mile Island and the tragic mass suicides at Jonestown. Many people were rejecting the old beliefs and searching for truth in Gurus and new religions. I was searching for truth in my own life, trying to sort out which path to follow.

This was a time of suffering and survival. It was during this time that I discovered something I called "floating your money." There were days when I had no money for gas to even drive to an interview. That's when I was forced to become creative. I remember when I was due a small paycheck on Friday from a temp job, but hadn't enough gas in my car to get to the job that day. So I stopped at a grocery store on Wednesday and, with only 78 cents in my account, wrote a check for five dollars. The store clerk said — "that's an awfully tiny check." I smiled and thought, *wait till tomorrow when it bounces and it'll be worth twenty bucks!*

I used the five dollars to put gas in my car. Then the next day I went to a second grocery store to write a check for another five dollars, which I put into my checking account to cover the first check. Then I deposited my small paycheck on Friday to cover the second check.

Another time I drove into a gas station on empty and asked the attendant if he would put gas in my car if I left my watch with him until I could come back with the money. He was nice enough to trust my word and helped me. He would not take the watch, but said I could pay him when I had the money. I went back that weekend to give him what I owed. God often sends his angels.

Women struggling to regain their prerogative as human beings, as well as the men who are themselves victims of their own abuse, need to open up to the courage of new growth; to step out on faith and place their vulnerable natures in God's hands. This is often a difficult task for those who have spent years learning to distrust, but it is the highest form of healing. No amount of therapy can heal the human soul like the Almighty Father, and the first step toward healing, I was discovering, is a humble heart. *Man's pride causes his humiliation, but he who is humble of spirit obtains honor. ~ Proverbs 29:23.*

Life is built upon moments. It's not the years that cause great changes in our lives, it's the moments. Those moments can be elating or devastating, but you know in that instant that your life has shifted once again and that tomorrow will be very different from yesterday.

I didn't know it at the time, but life was about to change, but this time, the change was welcomed. One evening I was in the kitchen going over the daily want ads when Joe, now thirteen, stood in the doorway, smiling. "What is it, Joe?"

"Someone's here," he said grinning.

"Who's here?

"Come see."

I walked into the living room to see a grown boy of sixteen, carrying a duffel bag and looking a bit uneasy. "Johnny?" I said softly. Somehow, in my mind I always pictured him as that nine-year-old boy I had grieved over for so long. Was this really that little boy? My heart was pounding so hard I could hardly get my breath. I could feel my knees trembling.

"Can I stay with you?" Johnny asked.

"Of course you can," I answered, blinking back tears.

It was so wonderful, but as incredible as it was to have him in my life after all those years, I instinctively realized it would not be easy for either of us. I didn't know Johnny and I was certainly a stranger to him. I wanted to run and put my arms around him. I didn't though. I could see he wasn't ready for that. So we just stood there staring at each other in silence and I knew this was a life-changing moment.

Since Joe's bed was small, we put blankets on the floor for Johnny. The boys rummaged through the trash rooms of the apartment project and came back with an old dresser someone had tossed out. Joe shared the floor with his brother that night. He couldn't stop smiling. I bent down and kissed them both good night. Johnny wasn't quite sure how to respond and I knew it would take time.

This was a dream come true and an answer to prayer, but I kept looking for traces of that nine-year-old. I still had the same love in my heart for him, but I realized that I knew very little about this teenage boy. Those missing years created a blind spot. I also knew that it must have been even more intense for Johnny — he really didn't know who I was. My identity was only a faded memory.

I was still out of a job, so Johnny got an evening job to help pay for his food. Even after I started working full-time, we had a long struggle financially. Times were so hard for the next few years that when Johnny graduated from high school he had to borrow a pair of dress shoes and a sport coat from a friend. I felt awful — angry with myself and with life. I wanted so much to give him a sense of security and to make up for those lost years. I had to keep reminding myself that God never promised us fair ... *but*, I thought, *he does promise us hope.*

I finally got a job. I had gone to an employment agency to see if they could find me a job and, ironically, the lady who interviewed me asked if I would consider working for her firm. Would I consider it? You bet I would! I accepted the job, and as an added bonus, there was no typing test. The work sounded interesting and I was so happy to have a job again. She explained that I would be contacting companies in search of open positions, then find the right person to fill that job. It was a sort of *talent hunt*. What I was to discover soon enough was that the hunt required me to be armed at all times.

#####

When I was very small, I would always call out at bedtime, "Granddaddy, come scratch my back." No matter what he was doing, the next thing I knew he was at my bedside, scratching my back. What a sense of peace and contentment that was for me. I could feel his love right down to my toes.

It's been wonderful when people have come along in my adult life to give me that sense of love and caring, even if it's only in the little things they do. Sometimes we just need someone to scratch our backs and let us know that we matter.

Chapter 13 **The Revolving Job Doors**

The following Monday I reported for work. As an Account Executive — a glorified title for headhunter — the glamour of my new job lasted one hour that first day. The "talent search" consisted of cold calling businesses to see if they had any job openings and then convincing them to use my services. I had to assure them of the many qualified candidates I had whom they would hire on sight. If I was fortunate enough to get a job order in the morning, then in the afternoon I had to cold call other companies to find someone looking for a new job, or who knew of someone who might be interested. Once I found a person, I needed to convince them to come to my office as soon as possible, before someone else filled the position.

I was always surprised when an applicant actually kept the appointment. I was curious to see what she was like. Was she intelligent, articulate, attractive and, did she have qualifying skills? Could she type? I never thought I'd ever ask that question of anyone. Over the phone, they would tell you anything you wanted to hear, but in person it was often quite different. So there I was in an extremely aggressive role where I had to succeed. My job paid a modest salary, but it was the commission that became my lifeline.

One ironic twist to this job was that, though there was a minimal amount of typing, I became the senior typist in the office. None of the other girls could type as well as I could. Imagine that! However, having been given that distinction, my typing improved considerably. It helped prove to me that as self-esteem develops, so do abilities. "You want something typed?" I would ask. "Sure, no problem!"

After a couple of weeks on the job, I got a revelation of things to come if I didn't make this job work for me. I saw women hired one morning and leave in tears the next morning. It was a tough business. The reason I was still there after two weeks was that I was terrified that I'd be the next one out the door, and there was no way I was going to let that happen. I began saying things to God like — "Do you really think I need this?" or — "When I asked you to make me stronger, this was not what I had in mind!"

However, no one realized my apprehensions. In fact, my boss held me up as an example. "Look at Peggy," he would say, "why she never lets the phone receiver leave her hand. She even works through lunch. Now that's the kind of aggressive behavior everyone should have." Aggressive behavior? Me? He didn't know I was simply scared to death of failing.

I managed to succeed and take control of my job. I was always amazed at the number of women who came in at my request. I became aware of how many people were unhappy with their jobs, even at the higher levels. One woman, who usually gave us job orders, had an enviable position with her company. She had a secure position and a good salary, but when one of my coworkers called in an effort to fill a high level position, the woman asked, "How about me? You can only serve your boss so many tuna on crackers."

I was getting so good at my job that during our morning pep talks I was occasionally asked to give a positive attitude talk to the office personnel. Things were looking good and I envisioned myself finally having enough money to do more than just survive. However, I didn't figure on the nation's economy taking a plunge into a recession. It was the early 1980s and suddenly the economy tilted and with it went my commission. It seemed to happen overnight. The very companies I had depended upon were now telling me they could no longer afford to pay us to find employees. They would need to search for them on their own.

Money was again becoming a huge problem. I could feel the

desperation growing inside me, although I prayed about it and tried as hard as I could to keep a positive attitude. Again I began devouring positive reading material. One evening I was home reading. The weather was terrible. It had been raining all day. The book I was reading expounded on the idea of the Law of Compensation: whatever you give to God will come back to you one hundred fold. I agreed that this was true. The book also stated "What you say is what you get." As the Bible says in Proverbs 6:2, "*You are snared by the words of your mouth.*" I agreed with that statement as well. I was feeling good about my positive affirmations when I heard the front door open. Johnny walked in looking guilty. Johnny had asked to use my car earlier in the evening, saying he wasn't going out of Greenbelt and wouldn't be gone long.

"What happened, John?" I asked cautiously.

"I didn't mean for it to happen, Mom, but it was raining so hard that when I turned the corner the car slid and … and hit the curb."

"Where is the car?"

"It's at the gas station. The impact bent the wheel. It's going to cost about $200 to fix. I'm really sorry."

My first reaction was to panic. I didn't know when I would have $200 and even if Johnny helped with the cost, it would take time to save up the money. All I could think of was getting to my job without a car. I would need to catch two buses and it would take a couple of hours one-way. I was really beginning to panic when I caught myself. I thought, *wait a minute, Peggy. You just read a book that reiterated what you already believe and you agreed that it spoke the truth. Now, if you really believe what you claim, then you will trust God to help you solve this problem. Just keep remembering — problems are for solving.*

I told Johnny not to worry — it would be okay. Then I

searched in my purse for the money I would need to take the bus to work. I counted the bus fare for the rest of the week until payday. I had two dollars left. I made up my mind that I was going to do what the Bible states in Malachi 3:10 — "*Put me to the test*," says the Lord, "*if I will not open the windows of heaven for you and pour down an overflowing blessing*." "All right, Lord, I'm gonna put you to the test just like you said."

The next day was Sunday and it was still raining so hard it looked like a river outside my window. I got dressed, put my two dollars in my coat pocket, and started walking to Mass. I was a little late getting to church and when I arrived the priest was speaking about the widow who put her last two pence in the collection basket. I thought, *how ironic*.

During the offertory, when the basket was passed, I placed my last two dollars in the collection basket and said to God: "I believe without a doubt that you are going to give this money back to me one hundred fold. I need your help, Lord, and I need it now. I thank you."

I walked home after Mass and when I got to my apartment I was soaked. I was drying my hair when the phone rang. It was my mother. She had just spoken with my brother, David, in California, and was so excited that she had to call me. It seemed my brother had finally gotten a good job after a lengthy search and wanted to do something for me. My mother said she wasn't supposed to tell me, but David had just put a check in the mailbox to me for $200!

"'*Put me to the test,' says the Lord*." I sat there and cried. It was so incredible and the Lord sure didn't waste any time in answering my prayer. When I told the priest at church what had happened, he asked, "Will you come to Mass next Sunday and put the check in the collection basket and try for double or nothing?"

"I don't think I'll push it." I laughed. "I just want to get my car on the road."

My paycheck began to reflect the new economic scene of the early `80s, which struck a brutal blow to the economy, and I wondered what might happen next. I didn't have long to wonder. Within a few weeks, a letter came from the Social Security Administration. The letter said I would no longer receive my benefits due to Government cutbacks. The benefits were to be cut immediately. Those benefits paid half of my rent. It was already two weeks into the month, which meant I had two more weeks to come up with the money to pay that month's rent. It also meant I had to come up with this amount for next month's rent and each month after that. One thing was certain — I couldn't do it on my present salary. I had to do something fast. Fear was a driving force for me in the `80s and began to propel me toward another change.

Someone told me about a company hiring telephone solicitors for evening and weekend work. The pay, even though it was partially based on commission, would pay the rent and buy food, if nothing else, and it would free me to search for another day job. Everything happened so quickly. I went for an interview one evening, was hired, and told to report to work the next evening. That's the kind of job it was. Of course, this meant going into the office the next morning to resign so I could start the new job that same evening. My current job with the employment agency didn't require prior notice, so it all fell into place, although leaving a job that quickly is difficult. No one, including myself, had a chance to go through the normal process of separation, and that was sad.

If I thought being a headhunter was stressful, I had no idea how stressful my evening job would be. I was given a script, which I had to repeat over and over verbatim for seven hours with only a ten-minute break. To make matters worse, we were monitored randomly and put on speaker periodically so everyone in the room could hear. We were given computer cards with names and phone numbers to call nationally, selling magazines and services. Amazingly, many people bought what I was selling. It was my job to complete the script without being stopped and, if I was interrupted, to overcome their objections with a second script. I was instructed to always end the conversation with — "okay?" This was to solidify the sale. I came to hate the word "okay."

There were many nights when I would leave the job at 1:00 am with a sore throat from trying to project my voice for those many hours, and my tongue would be bleeding from rubbing against my teeth as I continuously spoke. We were required never to put the phone on its cradle and to keep our dialing finger pushing those buttons endlessly because every minute counted.

During this time, I got a part-time day job in a shoe factory working on the accounting books. This job subsidized my evening salary and helped to keep us afloat, though I was getting behind in some payments. I also started looking for a full-time day job. A few weeks into my search, one of my former managers from the employment firm called to ask if I would like to interview with a company we had previously gone to for job orders. I was very thankful for her help.

The company was a financial institution for auto loans, which was located a few minutes from my home and a ten-minute drive to my evening job. I had gotten so far behind in my personal finances that, for a while, I would need to keep the evening job to get solvent. I began working from 8:30 in the morning to 5:00 p.m. on my day job and went straight to my night job, working from 5:30 to 1:00 a.m. I usually had one and, occasionally, a second night off a week, and worked nine hours either a Saturday or Sunday. I worked both jobs for about eight months. When I walked out of the telephone-soliciting job for the last time, I was ecstatic, although I could never complain. It provided for me when I needed it so desperately.

I was hoping I had found my niche on my new job with the financial firm, but I was soon to wonder if I even had a niche. I discovered that working for the finance corporation was another tough spot. It paid the bills but, not without assaulting my integrity. I often worked overtime without compensation because I took my job seriously and wanted to succeed. I remember one January walking a mile through a heavy snowstorm because I lived closer than anyone else and they needed to get the contracts out. I cared about my job and wanted to do it well. I gave it everything I had, believing that, if I gave my best, I'd be rewarded for my efforts — the Law of Compensation. Just the opposite happened. I was still vulnerable and sadly there are people who delight in taking advantage of vulnerability.

#####

I guess one of the luxuries I recall about being a small child was Grandmother's feather bed. Just before she was ready for bed, she'd ask if I wanted to fluff up her feather mattress and be the first one to dive in. She had only to ask once. I would fluff it up until it was a huge mountain of feathers, soft and plump. Then I'd jump into the air and land right in the middle. It felt like one of those puffy clouds you see in the sky on warm summer days. I lay there, not wanting to break the spell. I used to wonder if that's what a cloud felt like, but I figured I would have to die to find out, so I was quite content with the feather bed. Much later in life I would wonder if Grandma was plumping up a cloud in heaven for a good night's sleep. "I hope it's as comforting as your feather bed, Grandma."

Chapter 14 **The Sproutland**

One Friday afternoon, my manager asked if I would work that Saturday. Any other time I would have agreed, but that particular weekend I was going on a retreat with a group of women from my church and had already paid for the weekend. I was also responsible for providing the music for the retreat. I told the manager about my plans. He said nothing, and I gave it no more thought, but when I came to work the following Monday, one of my co-workers whispered to me, "Be careful. When you didn't work on Saturday they went through your desk drawers to see if they could find anything to write you up."

"What do you mean, write me up?"

"You know, when they write you up they put down anything they can find that they don't like and it goes in your file and on your permanent record."

"But I haven't done anything. What could they possibly say?"

"All I know is that they found some filing in a folder that you hadn't completed and that's what they intend to use."

"That doesn't make any sense. No one has time to keep up with the filing. That's something you do whenever you can; when you've managed to get the important things accomplished."

"Maybe so, but I'm warning you," she said softly, "be careful."

It didn't take very long to realize what she said was true. The supervisor came over to my desk and asked me to step into the head manager's office with him. I followed him and, once inside, they asked me to have a seat. The manager was very pleasant and said, "Over the weekend Steve found a folder that belongs to you. Seems it contains some filing that should have been put in the files. I mean, what if someone needed to look for it?"

"I don't understand," I said curiously. "I was told when I came to work here that the filing is never completed because we need to spend our time on contracts and credit checks, and those things can't always be accomplished in an eight-hour day. That's why many nights I'm here until 6 or 7, and I don't get paid for what I do past five o'clock. Why are you doing this? Was it because I didn't agree to work on Saturday?"

"Look, these are the rules. Now, we just ask you to sign this paper stating you're sorry for not completing your work as scheduled and that you won't do it again. That's all. Okay?"

"No, it's not okay," I bristled. "I have done nothing wrong and I'm not going to sign a paper saying I have."

"If you don't, we're going to come down very hard on you." Steve warned.

"Well, be that as it may, I'm not signing your paper. I haven't done anything wrong and I am not going to say that I have."

So, after what I felt was a good job performance, I was demoted to a job that no one wanted. It was boring, tedious and stifling. To make matters worse, and to show by example that I was being punished for my mistakes, they separated my desk from everyone else. I couldn't understand this treatment. I always took my jobs seriously and gave all I had to give, and I worked at keeping a good attitude. But I was determined not to sink back into the old feelings of despair. I would not allow myself to feel like the victim again. A verse by Henry Thoreau kept running through my mind, "In the spring I burned over a hundred acres till the earth was sere and black, and by mid-summer this space was clod in a fresher and more luxuriant green than the surrounding even. Shall man then despair? Is he not a sproutland, too, after ever so many searings and witherings?"

I was going to be a "sproutland" and I would find another job that would bring me hope and opportunities. The Bible says in Psalms 37:5, "*Commit your way to the Lord; trust in him, and he will act*." I would believe, even as I sat at my desk and the tears trickled down my cheeks, that God would not let this go on without revealing a better way. "Dear, Father, get me out of here, please ... and soon."

Within two days I received a call at work from Joleen, a friend who lived in the Baltimore area. She and her husband, Pierre, had attended a party where, Fran, a friend of theirs happened to mention that her company was opening a branch office in my area and was looking for a branch administrator. They mentioned that I was looking for a new job. The next day Fran called me at work to say I would need to drop off my resume to the branch office by the next evening.

"No problem," I said with much eagerness. "I'll have it there."

I interviewed two days later. That Friday, I received another phone call. "We would like to hire you as our branch administrator in the new office. Will you accept the job?"

I almost stood on my desk and shouted, "Yes, yes! When can I start?"

Forgiveness is not always easy, but I knew I didn't want bitterness to build inside me. I also knew that though I found it difficult to forgive the people who had hurt me so deeply, I could begin by asking God to soften my heart and to open me to the feelings he wanted to place there. I realized that there is always a trade-off in everything we do. What was the trade-off for holding onto my anger? Once I discovered that it was resentment, motivated by retaliation, I was able to move on. But not without one small point of reprisal. I hadn't planned it. It just happened. But I must admit, it gave me a sense of power after the many weeks of feeling powerless.

One of the supervisors was a man not yet twenty-five who had married an older woman who was the daughter of a top manager in the company. All the men working there seemed to be in competition with each other to show they were tough enough to deserve corporate recognition. This man evidently felt he had even more to prove.

He would pile stacks of papers a foot high on my desk and then ask when I thought I would have the work completed. Of course, I could never determine a time. There was too much work to have any idea how long it would take me. However, he would press for an answer. When I finally gave him a tentative time, he would put pressure on me to have it done by then.

On the day I was to hand in my resignation, this young supervisor was in a particularly critical mood. When I had been demoted, I also lost the use of my computer, so whenever I needed to look up information I had to go to someone else and ask if they would stop their work long enough to allow me to turn their computer around so I could use it. This day I had a few items to research and had asked one of the women if I could use her computer for about five minutes. When I sat down at her computer, I noticed the supervisor watching me closely. I could see him moving toward me out of the corner of my eye. The coworker asked me a question. I answered briefly, but never stopped the computer search to talk. I was aware that the supervisor had moved closer and was standing just a few feet away.

He suddenly bellowed, "Peggy, when will you have that work ready for me?" His tone was most condescending.

What he didn't know was that I had my resignation in my desk drawer ready to turn in at closing that day. Something snapped inside me. I'm sure it was because I had nothing to lose. I was out of there and I didn't even need a recommendation from them.

Without looking up from the computer, I said slowly and deliberately, in a voice that could be heard throughout the huge computer room, "You'll get your work when I'm damn good and ready...okay?"

He uttered a weak, "okay," and walked off. I'm sure he went straight to management to tell them of my insubordination. Once he was safely out of the room, all computer activity came to a halt. The employees peered in unison around their computers to give me a silent applause, whispering softly, "hurrah!" I guess I had said what they had wanted to say, but were too afraid they'd lose their jobs.

Later I told God, "It was just one moment of vindictiveness. That's all it was. Now you can work on softening my heart, *okay*?" I told him meekly.

Over the years I have given much time to contemplating life. I know that one of our missions on earth is to discover some of the secrets of life. I suppose that's the reason I spent as much time as I could alone. It was at those times when only God and me were present to each other that the great truths of my existence were revealed; even if I didn't realize I was in the presence of God. Somehow having the courage to be alone for an extended period of time produces growth.

I was beginning to finally benefit from all the years of studying life. I felt I was opening up to the uniformity of God's Laws. I was beginning to realize that when our personal world is thrown into change, be it good or adverse change, it is our responsibility to work toward a new balance. And it is in recovering our balance that we find God's will for us, especially in dark times when we are forced to search for the truth in ourselves. That's where balance comes into play. I had so many inner conflicts. I seemed to be a myriad of different people inside. It was all so confusing. Then I thought about my whole lineage down the centuries, all those people who contributed to who I am as a person. Maybe that's where part of the confusion came from. Maybe not all the conflicting feelings were my own — I borrowed them from the past. I realized that I needed to deal with the conflicts, but to choose my battles. When I tried to solve them all, I became overwhelmed. So I took the feelings that were most important and worked on them, leaving the rest behind until later. In my continuing need to know myself, I was to discover that every day is another opportunity to redefine my identity.

I felt I had stretched my capacity to discover stability in my life. Instinctively, I knew that falling too far off balance meant emotional difficulties. I also realized that when I refused to face the dark times, I experience denial, and growth does not come from denial. It is in accepting and dealing with suffering that I would discover who I was at that particular moment and what I needed to do to regain my emotional equilibrium. Each time I tried to hide from the truth or avoid my pain, I got off balance, and because it added more pain and produced feelings of guilt and self-loathing — I quickly began to work on finding a measure of stability once more. I truly felt I was trying to balance life on the edge of a cliff. I found that we all have a built-in gauge to work with, and I needed so much to feel good about myself.

#####

My grandparents lived next to a big wooded area when I was young and that's where I spent a good deal of my time, especially in the summer months. I went there to be alone with God, although, at that time, he was just a feeling. There was so much peace and tranquility in the forest. I could feel the hand of God all around me.

I realized as I left my job that last day, that the forest was where I actually began to feel like a *sproutland after so many searings and witherings.*

Chapter 15 **Grow Where You Are Planted**

Life has a way of putting us where we can learn and grow. I have heard time and again the old adage, "grow where you are planted." As trite as the old maxims may sound, they still hold truisms of validity for our lives. When I started my job with the computer consultant firm, I truly began to "grow where I was planted." It was a brand new company, a sort of "mom and pop" outfit. I felt right away that it was a sound company of quality and professionalism. The company hired computer programmers who worked on temporary assignments for clients. These client corporations preferred this arrangement rather than hiring employees.

I was so excited the day I started my new job and looked forward to the challenges. I was not disappointed. Each week I traveled to the Towson, Maryland, headquarters where Phyllis, my mentor, went over the instructions for the week. Then I would take that knowledge back to my office, along with bountiful notes to reference, and endeavored to put all of it into perspective. Phyllis was a stern taskmaster and a good teacher. I appreciated her skills and absorbed everything she told me with gusto. It was a pleasure to have someone knowledgeable willing to share that knowledge. I was so used to figuring out by trial and error what a job required, so all the challenges Phyllis assigned I met with enthusiasm and excitement. Learning was such a pleasure and there seemed no end to what was expected of me, or how I had to stretch to meet those expectations. I realized during those years that when management has high expectations of an employee and those anticipations are coupled with supportive strength and an affirming approach, success is the end result.

I was impressed with Walda, the branch manager, even before I met her, when I heard that upon being asked where she got the experience to run a branch office, she said it was from raising her children. I knew I would like her down-to-earth approach.

When hiring our secretary, I interviewed several people to no avail. That's when I decided to utilize the skills I had developed while working for the employment agency. I simply picked up the phone and cold called companies until I came across someone who knew a young girl wanting to advance, but could go no further in her present job. Margaret was a delight. She had an almost gullible honesty. One day the office phone rang, and I heard Margaret say: "Walda can't come to the phone right now. She's eating an orange." She soon learned to be a little less frank when answering the phone, but what she lacked in professionalism when first hired, she more than made up for with her positive attitude and hard work. Within the branch, we developed a great team of people who worked well together.

The founders of the company were fairly new in business and still learning to run a company successfully. All of the newly formed branches worked closely with the corporate office. There was a feeling of camaraderie. Fran, the administrator for all the branch offices, worked out of corporate headquarters. Fran was firm in her approach, but under her management, the branch administrators applied themselves and delivered successful job performances. She expected the best and the best is what we gave.

Because the company was newly formed, there were constant changes in the structure of the work. As soon as it became a familiar routine, the routine changed. I had to become very flexible. It seemed that as a concept became familiar it was time to try it another way, but I never resisted the changes. I found them instead to be stimulating. I was beginning to learn that non-resistance to change creates a wider learning curve and expands our capacity to comprehend. I allowed those changes to change me, and kept my attitude open-ended.

The company gave me much latitude for creativity. I devised new forms and procedures that the company adopted for use universally in all the branch offices. I was appreciated for my originality and it felt good to be part of a growing company where my best was not only expected but also esteemed. I began to stretch and expand in order to comply with those expectations. The more they asked, the more I stretched. I was beginning to realize that I could do a multitude of things and do them well, and my self-confidence excelled.

I was responsible for all the branch office reports, many of which had tight deadlines. I conducted administrative orientations for new employees, explaining the benefits and company policies. I was the contact person between the clients and our employees and it was my job to solve the problems of those employees working in the field and to keep them well informed — a bit like being the mother to fifty offspring.

I facilitated evening classes and, on occasion, created some class material. I was totally responsible for the annual Christmas party for our client corporations and our employees. It was an awesome task and required planning over the entire year, since these galas were expected to be elegant and unique from year to year. My job required much of me in a very short time. I was determined to do my best and loved the challenges.

This was an eventful time in my private life, too. Johnny and Joe were now out on their own. Johnny stayed in the area but Joe ventured to California to stay with Debralee while he pursued opportunities to enhance his talent for music.

My father died in 1987 of a sudden heart attack. A special bond had grown between us. I was thankful we had been given the opportunity to know and appreciate each other before that fateful day. My father never spoke of his former years, but I'm certain he was grateful to have the chance to be part of our family.

My father had always said that when he died, he wanted a funeral with full military honors and to be buried in Arlington Cemetery. I discovered upon his death that there was no room for further burials in the cemetery but, if cremated, he could be entombed in one of the burial walls. I wasn't sure what I should do, but finally decided that if cremation was my only option in following his wishes, this is what I would do. As it turned out, the ceremony was done with great dignity and honor, and I know Daddy would have been pleased.

My mother and I reached a pinnacle stage in our relationship although, at the time, I didn't realize what was happening. My mother was an interesting character. She loved being with people and could out talk anyone. I remember entering the waiting room of her doctor's office with her as she said, "I don't feel like getting into a big conversation with anyone today, but just watch, someone will want to talk to me. It happens everywhere I go. People always start conversations with me."

So I thought — okay, I can relate to feeling that way. Sometimes that's just the way a person feels. But I knew my mother, and I waited to see what she would do. I didn't have long to wait. She sat quietly for a few minutes and then suddenly said to the person sitting across from her, "Don't you just hate this weather?" The other person commented, and my mother coaxed, "What are you here for?" I thought, *for someone who doesn't feel like talking, Mama's hardly keeping a low profile.*

My mother also had a way of getting her point across without verbal communication. She had asked her medical doctor for a recommendation regarding the dentist who occupied an office in the same building. The doctor said he knew him well and that he was a fine dentist, so on the doctor's advice, my mother began extensive dental work, which included dentures. The teeth never fit correctly even after the dentist filed them down and used other procedures. She let the doctor know that the dentist he had recommended was not satisfactory. To which the doctor replied sternly that as far as he knew, the recommendation was a good one. So on future visits to the doctor, rather than complain about the dentist, Mother simply took out her false teeth and began to file them down in the presence of the doctor. The doctor, so as to get his point across, proceeded to check her chart and hum to himself. They never discussed the dentist, but each knew exactly how the other felt about the subject.

My mother and I began a process that was totally new to us and it escalated quickly. At the time, it felt like the worst period in our relationship. Actually, in retrospect, it was beneficial to both of us because it opened up an honest discourse for the first time. My mother was a good person, but she really never grew up and didn't want to. When she moved back from California, I realized she was here to recapture her past, her youth, the parties she remembered so well. In her mind, she was not aging — the people in California had changed. They weren't fun anymore. They were settled now and wanted to grow old gracefully. She believed that in returning to the East Coast, she could pick up where she had left off twenty years earlier. It was devastating to her to find out that the people she remembered from a more youthful time were themselves getting on in age and didn't want to party anymore. The party was over.

Although her senior citizen's building offered many social events, my mother eventually cut herself off more and more from her peers. Following a lengthy hospital stay after a broken hip, she refused to allow anyone in her apartment, even the visiting nurse for which I had arranged. She wanted only me. She would tell me that she wanted us to be constant companions, as she remembered a friend and her daughter from California. "They wanted no one but each other," she would say.

I knew I disappointed her because I didn't want what she wished for. I didn't want a narrow life. I wanted more. Curiously, I believe that in my marriage I had been confronted with a similar challenge of wills; a challenge to cut myself off from humanity, from life, — and now, it seemed my mother's quest was to capture my singular attention and devotion. She was a strong personality and preferred me standing in her shadow. Again, what I felt and what I desired was not considered.

Mother wanted me to fill the emptiness she felt inside and I couldn't, though I wanted to see her happy. After she broke her hip and came home to recuperate, I complied as best I could by spending every evening with her until her bedtime. Over the years I had become, as she put it, "her seamstress, her financial aide, her nurse, her chauffeur, her cook, her everything." I didn't want to be her everything, although I couldn't tell her. For as long as I could remember I had seen my mother as bigger than life. It was confusing, for on the one hand, I knew she was a wonderful person, a great friend to people. This was evident. But, I also knew that she did not understand parenting. Being a parent meant being a responsible adult and, while she gave love, which was most important, she did not take on responsibilities.

My mother had a keen intellect. She could have done anything she wanted in life had she only possessed the discipline. Instead, I remember her constantly saying, "I want to be waited on hand and foot like the rich." And in the last years of her life, she got her wish, but unfortunately it was not as the lady of leisure, but because of her incapacitation.

#####

My maternal grandparents had been married only a short while when my grandmother discovered she was pregnant with my mother. My grandfather, who was twenty years old at the time, worked for the railroad and daily helped to run thc train through the small town. There was a high bridge above the tiny house where Benjamin and Sudie lived. Each morning, Benjamin would blow the train whistle as he passed over the bridge and Sudie would eagerly run to the window to wave as he passed by. Then one morning, feeling ill because of her pregnancy, she heard the train approach and the whistle wail, but she didn't go to the window. That morning Benjamin fell from the train to his death. My grandmother was six months into her pregnancy.

Chapter 16 **The Confrontation**

I was beginning to realize that I had become a coconspirator in my mother's secret life of drinking. I finally refused to go to the liquor store for her, but it didn't matter, because she found stores that would deliver to her door. I tried talking to her doctor, but my mother denied she had a problem, so he seemed confused over whom to believe. Evenings when I would leave her place, she would reach into the closet and pull out a bag with an empty wine bottle inside, wrapped in newspaper and tied with cord. She would whisper, afraid the neighbors might hear, that she could no longer put the bottles in the trash bin of her building because they would know the bottles belonged to her. She urged me to take them home and throw them in my dumpster. I protested, but in the end, I gave in, knowing it made no sense and feeling like an enabler.

Once again, world news told us how vulnerable we were as horror unfolded with the explosive destruction of the reactor at the Soviet Union's Chernobyl power plant, unleashing a radioactive cloud for miles. I paralleled those times in my own reactions to life's stresses, a reaction that unleashed the power of my own meltdown.

It was during Mama's period of recuperation after hip surgery that we were thrown together in a constant battle of wills. I had never stood up to my mother. I kept it all inside. I felt that a daughter didn't have the right to speak out against a parent and, when it finally happened, I discovered the world did not come to a halt, my mother did not curl up retching with pain, and I was not struck down by the wrath of God.

Through the summer months Mama repeatedly pushed the limits. I wonder now if, somewhere inside her, she was unconsciously testing me. Maybe she instinctively knew I was a stronger person inside than I revealed and, because of her failing health, she needed a strong person to lean on. I doubt that she knew this on a conscious level, but I believe she was led to this not only for herself, but for me as well. It was a definite turning point in both our lives.

Many evenings she would ask if I were hungry. I wasn't. She would insist that I was. I held my ground. I was anything but hungry. One particular evening, she asked me to get some items for her from the grocery store. I returned to find that she had made me a peanut butter sandwich. For someone who had said she could not get out of bed for any reason, she somehow managed to get into her wheelchair and out to the kitchen to prepare the sandwich. As in the past, my feelings and desires were not considered. In previous times, I would have eaten the sandwich rather than confront the situation. What really brought things to a head was that it was a peanut butter sandwich and I had not been able to tolerate peanut butter since childhood; peanut butter would gag me. Had she been there during those years, she would have known this. It's the little things that mold our lives — the happenings we don't plan — these are the moments that change lives forever. That night both our lives changed because of a peanut butter sandwich.

"I can't eat peanut butter," I asserted. She insisted that I eat the sandwich — that, "I know what's best for you." That started a series of verbal confrontations that brought all the previous years to a head. Many evenings I would leave her apartment frustrated and angry, get in my car, put the windows up and scream. I had to get it out. Sometimes I even yelled at God.

What really brought things to a head was when she said she was happy she had given birth to me because — as she put it, "Who would do for me now?" That did it. I confronted her with all the repressed hurts gathered over the years. I must admit I watched for her reaction and tried to be gentle, but firm — very firm. Had she seemed overly disturbed by what I was saying, I would have ceased the onslaught but, to my surprise, she was much too resilient for that. It seemed to be a healing start for both of us. I was completely honest, and it was extremely hard.

Some weeks into her recuperation, it became apparent that my mother was simply vegetating and doing nothing to help herself, so her doctor made arrangements for her to enter a nursing facility. Again, I felt guilty as if I had failed her. But to my surprise, she changed for the positive the very first day she was admitted. She became the social person she had been her whole life. In her apartment she would not get out of bed or get dressed. In the nursing center she was the first one up in the morning, dressed, and ready for breakfast. She became the effusive person she had been before. But she needed constant supervision and attention. Most of all, she needed the discipline they could give. But with all of this came a shift in roles. I became the mother and she became the daughter, and she was becoming an unruly child. The nurses would call me at work with complaints such as — "We caught your mother smoking in the girl's room again," or "Your mother refuses to take her bath unless you are here." So I would ask them to put her on the phone and told her that if she did not do what was expected of her, I would not come down on the weekend. She could be very trying, but once confronted, she complied.

I remember waiting in the hospital emergency room with her one day when she found out she wasn't allowed to smoke in the hospital. She sat in the wheelchair and pleaded with every nurse who came by to please push her outdoors for a few minutes. "If I could only feel the sun on my shoulders once again," she would plead. But I knew what she was really craving, and it wasn't the sunshine.

I continued to do what I could to make her life a positive experience. I went to the nursing home every weekend and would take her for drives or to lunch and, if the weather permitted, push her wheelchair along the path so we could enjoy the spring flowers and the buds on the trees. Somehow I understood what she was all about, and because she had finally allowed me my anger, I could be much more sympathetic toward her. Everything in life is a trade-off. It is always a give and take and that word "balance" comes into play over and over. For our relationships to work, we need to allow for a healthy exchange. Compromise promotes forgiveness and gives each person a chance to develop some personal power. There is something quite devastating about feeling powerless in a relationship. We are all created equal under God, and no one has the right to take away that liberty. It is our responsibility to make sure that we enter into relationships to promote growth and cooperate with God in co-creating ourselves, and we must allow our loved ones to do the same. At this time in my life, I was truly becoming aware of my collaboration with God.

#####

When I was growing up, I could see how different life was for those who had personal power in their lives. They had a command of life. But I could also see what it was like when power was used to hurt others. I remember World War II and the way it changed people. Everyone seemed to be more afraid. The innocence I once associated with life had changed abruptly. After that, innocence for all of us became evasive.

I had recaptured that feeling of innocence again behind the safety of the convent walls. Now, it escaped me once again, as I felt the thunder of my personal wars lurking on the horizon.

Chapter 17 **<u>Mountains Are For Moving</u>**

I continued to work for the computer consultant firm for over five years. It was stimulating, I liked the people, and I was recognized for my worth as a person and as an employee. Our branch office was fun. Harry, one of the salespeople, had a wonderful way of setting the tone for the office. Harry was never discouraged no matter what seemed to go wrong in his life. I learned a lot about resilience from him. Harry, as well as Pat, Dennis, and Mike helped to create a warm and family-like atmosphere.

My only complaint about the company was the salary structure for those in clerical positions. My rent, car insurance and other bills increased at a higher rate each year than my salary increases. When this happens, you begin to slip backwards into a measurable recession. There were times when I took on extra work to make up the difference.

Cars were often a challenge. I managed to take care of my regular expenses, but upkeep on a second-hand car was an added expense I could seldom afford. As a result, I did little in the way of preventive maintenance, other than oil changes. I remember over a period of months hearing a creaking noise whenever I took a left turn. Because the car was old, I figured the noise was just that — old age. One evening I had a flat tire on the front driver's side and was close enough to pull into a gas station to have my spare tire put on. Had it been any other tire, I wouldn't have had the warning that my car had a serious problem. Nor would I have been warned of this danger if the spare tire had not had a slow leak. Every few days I stopped at a service station to put air in my tire. Because of this, I finally decided that I simply had to purchase a new tire. I took the car in and within a few minutes of removing the old tire, the mechanic paged me to come to the service bay. He was shaking his head as I approached. “Do you know how lucky you are?” he asked. “The whole ball joint was cracked and when I took the tire off, the joint snapped in half. If you had been traveling on the road when that happened it would have caused a terrible accident.” I was stunned. How many months had I heard that creaking noise? All I could think was — thanks for the warning, Lord.

Within that same year, repairs on my car became imperative, but the car was too old for costly maintenance. It finally breathed its last and I was without a car for six months. I had no money for a down payment, nor could I afford a car payment each month. In the meantime, I rode the bus to and from work. Finally, I bought a car that had been used by the dealership as a loner car. They said they were selling it to me as a new car and any problems would be repaired to my satisfaction. So, on that premise, I purchased the car. However, when I took possession of the car and was on the way home, I became aware that something was wrong. The brakes did not work properly and when I tried to stop the car it pulled hard to one side. The steering was rough and the brakes caused the car to shimmy. When I arrived home, I called the dealership to say I wanted someone to look the car over — that I wasn't satisfied with its performance.

I had bought the car in good faith and I took it back believing the dealership would stand behind the company's word. The immediate reaction from the service manager was, “What did you do to the car on your way home? You must have hit something,” he accused. “The rim of the front wheel and the rotor are both bent.” I couldn't understand. I had always believed that people would treat you fairly if you confronted them honestly. Somehow this wasn't working. The service manager refused to listen to me.

I was tired of being pushed around. I decided to write a letter to Lee Iacocca at the automobile corporation. It didn't take long before I received a letter and a phone call from the company telling me that the dealership would make good the repairs on my car. I had also asked to be provided a rental car during the duration of the repair work and the letter stated I would indeed be given a rental car. I was most grateful. It took almost a month for the dealer to repair my car, so I was happy to have the rental car in the interim, even though that first morning the engine wouldn't start and I had to get a jump-start that cost me $7.50. The dealer said I would be reimbursed for this expense when I picked up my car.

When the repairs were completed, I went to the dealership to pick up my car. The mechanic wrote up the ticket and told me calmly that I owed $831.00. "Wait a minute," I confronted, "I am not supposed to pay anything for this work." All I could think of was the $15.00 I had in my checking account. I asked to see the manager who had approved the repairs. I was told he was in Florida. I asked if someone would call him there. I was told that they didn't have a number where he could be reached. I tried to explain the situation, but he was not listening. I finally did something I had never done before. I made a spectacle of myself. I started yelling that the dealership had sold me a car with faulty brakes and that I should have taken it to the police station on the way home that day, since the dealer obviously didn't care about my safety. I said another letter would be going to the corporation. All the customers were staring. The mechanic said softly, "Wait here, I'll be back in a minute."

A few minutes later he came back smiling, waving some coupons. "Look at this," he said, "we're gonna give you a rebate worth $200."

"You don't understand," I repeated, "I am not to pay anything for this work!"

Again, he left and when he came back he had two rebates. I

carefully reiterated, "No rebates — no charge."

Again, he left the service bay and was gone quite a while. When he came back he was red in the face. He obviously didn't want to deal with me any longer. He stuffed a receipt in my hand and said, "Here, take your car and go home."

"No charge?"

"No charge," he scoffed, "just take your car and go home."

What a relief! I was so happy. There was just one more thing to take care of before leaving. I pulled from my purse the $7.50 receipt for the expense of the jump-start on their rental car. "What about this?" I asked.

"Just step to the cashier and she'll take care of it!" He said through his teeth.

I was learning to fight for myself. I was confronting more situations, finding that I didn't have to look to myself alone for blame when something went wrong. I trusted my internal gauge to know when I was wrong in my thinking. I realized that often people project their own inner weaknesses and feelings of contempt onto others to relieve their feelings about themselves because of a poor self image. While we have a responsibility to help each other, we are not required to do it at the expense of our own integrity.

I had so much to be thankful for. Growth and change are sometimes painful — but after going through the changes and the spurts of growth, I knew I was a different person than before. I was stronger, wiser and more perceptive.

I am always amazed at those times when God gives direct answers to my prayers in such a way that I cannot doubt that those answers are from him. One example came during a stormy January when we had a substantial snowfall and, two days later, before the chance to dig out, another heavy snow fell. I took the bus to work that morning because the snow was already getting heavy. Around 11:00 the corporate office called to say I should close the office and go home. I was the only one in the office so I locked up and headed for the Metro bus terminal. When I arrived, there were nearly a hundred people waiting. I asked someone if the buses where running. I was told they had not picked up passengers for an hour. The bus drivers were dropping passengers off as they came into Metro Center, displaying the "not in service" sign, and driving away without picking up the people who were waiting.

It was a heavy, icy snow. I could feel it penetrating right through my coat. The wind blew so hard that ice pellets hit me in the face like stinging bullets. I looked around and saw a blind man who had been waiting for some time. He looked cold and distressed. I was so cold that my feet were frozen and I could hardly walk. By 2:00, after waiting three hours, I was desperate. I just wanted to go home. I had never been that cold in my life. I was so cold that my whole body hurt. I turned to God. I had been reading about thanking God for our prayer requests even before receiving an answer. The Bible says in Matthew 17:20 "*If you have faith as a grain of mustard seed, you shall say unto this mountain, remove hence to yonder place; and it shall remove, and nothing shall be impossible unto you.*" *Okay*, I thought, *somehow I have to move this mountain.*

I began to pray silently. For half an hour I repeated over and over under my breath, with all the emotion I could find inside me, "*Thank you, God, for the Greenbelt bus...thank you, God, for the Greenbelt bus...*" At 2:30, a bus pulled into Metro Center, right up to where all of us were standing. The driver opened the door and let his passengers off the bus. Then he began to rotate the sign on the display until it read: GREENBELT. Everyone looked at each other. Then someone asked, "are you gonna let us on?" The bus driver answered, "I must be crazy. I should go home like all the other drivers have done in this mess, but something keeps telling me to make one more trip to Greenbelt." I sighed deeply and said one more time, "*Thank you, God, for the Greenbelt bus.*"

The bus driver knew he was taking a real chance going to Greenbelt. What normally would have taken fifteen minutes to get out of Silver Spring, took two hours. And what would normally have taken one hour to Greenbelt took five more hours. When the bus driver went up a steep hill he asked us to get off the bus and walk to the top of the hill. Once he struggled to get the bus up the hill, we boarded again. When he came to a steep incline and was afraid he couldn't get the bus safely down the hill, he went to a private home to ask if he could call for a sand truck to go down in front of us.

The blind man had two other people get off at his stop and they helped him find his way home. Everyone on the bus was exhausted but grateful to the man who "had to make one more trip to Greenbelt." I didn't get the bus driver's name but I wrote down the number of the bus and called Metro the next day. I told them the driver had done more than most people would have even considered. He was a real hero and deserved some recognition and perhaps a bonus.

I was amazed at what God will do through us when we call on him in real need. It was as if I had reached out and touched the Infinite and the Infinite had reached back and lifted us on his shoulders. The mountain we couldn't get over, God had moved.

#####

Trust is a lifeline for we humans. We can endure many things if we trust the people who are helping us. Fear and trust can't co-exist. As a small child, I would often jump from the stairs, convinced that Granddad would catch me in his arms. I had no fear, because I trusted he would not let me fall. Now I put my trust in God. I know he will catch me if I fall — even if I must jump.

Chapter 18 **The Threads of Life**

"All human interactions are opportunities either to learn or to teach." M. Scott Peck, M.D., wrote this in his wonderful book, *The Road Less Traveled.* I was beginning to appreciate this truth. I was also beginning to realize that one reason we don't allow ourselves growth is that we're not willing to cultivate a new identity. We hold on securely to protect "who we are" — or rather — "who we think we are." And in holding on, we hinder life's *gift of change.* Maybe we are all afraid of the responsibilities that come with changing our identity. The greater the awareness, the greater the expectations.

During this time, the more I prayed for guidance, the more my world seemed to topple. There were so many times when I simply wanted to dig in my heels and say, "no more!" I wanted to get into a comfortable rut and glide. I wanted *time* to wait before challenging me again. But I seldom got my way.

I did a lot of running after *time* in the more than five years I worked for the consultant firm. I was expected to be time efficient and every moment counted for something. I learned to hold my concentration amid constant interruptions. I learned to deal with whatever the moment presented. I learned another lesson on the vulnerability of life the day I stood in front of the TV screen in our office as we watched the exciting liftoff of the space shuttle *Challenger.* However, my elation rapidly changed to disbelief as an explosion vaporized the remains of Shuttle Mission 51-L. All I could think of were the families of these brave pioneers who were watching this turn of events, and of the children around the country who lost their innocence in that moment. I realized all over again that life is too short to spend it in fear and doubt, and the vehicle in which we are traveling through life could vaporize in an instant.

The people who came in and out of my life during that period had a great impact upon me as a person. Those whom I admired, I learned from. There is a saying that goes: "What we love, we shall grow to resemble." I was grasping on a deeper level what it meant to teach and to learn from one another; how this give and take can actually change our direction through the inspiration of those we have come to love and trust.

In the middle of my fourth year of employment I could feel subtle changes beginning to stir within the company. The branch manager left to work in our Towson headquarters, and our secretary got a job with more advancement opportunities. Tracey came through a temp agency and stayed on for a couple of years as our secretary. Although Tracey was twenty years my junior, we thought very much alike and, at times, words were not even needed because we could get our thoughts across with a look or a smile. We simply clicked.

Ted, the new branch manager, was an interesting character. On the surface he appeared quite serious and a bit snobbish. Underneath all of that, however, was someone who enjoyed having fun — as long as he didn't have to acknowledge it. Tracey and I, realizing this, would do things like draping his chair during the holidays with Christmas lights and hanging a sign on the back that read: Electric chair! For his birthday, the whole office debated about what we should do. Ted had warned that he didn't want anyone spending money on him. Ted didn't believe in spending money on anything. I was sent out shopping to find some small gag gift. After much searching I found the perfect gift — a two-foot tall, chartreuse-colored plastic pig — a bank — into which we placed one penny. To everyone's surprise, he loved that pig.

And there was the time we put half a chocolate donut in his desk drawer. Later, Tracey found it in her purse, and when Ted went to the Philly branch for a week, we sent it to him in a mailing bag. He never mentioned any of the things we did to tease him, but he enjoyed them.

My job no longer held the same interest for me. A larger firm was assuming the company, the principals of the original company were planning to vacate, and the personal touch that I had grown to love was dissipating. It was time to move on. I began to send off my resume.

I could feel my job interest waning with each week that passed, feeling lethargic and bored. I was ready for the next step but didn't know what that step was to be. I had only received responses from a few resumes I sent out, and even with those interviews, nothing seemed to come together. I had to gather up all my self-discipline to continue in my job. Amazingly, in doing so, I found I was able to manufacture enough enthusiasm to do the job effectively and to keep the spirits up of the people working in the field. They no longer had that personal touch from management and so they relied on me for support. I couldn't allow my feelings to get in the way. Some of these employees were new and needed a sense of involvement and stability, and I was again allowing life to change me.

My last job interview fell through, because the girl I was to replace decided not to quit her job after all. I was becoming discouraged when someone suggested that I try writing down what I wanted in a job, placing it in my Bible, and praying about it. I thought it was a great idea. I wrote: Success and Fulfillment in My Work —

I desire to be fulfilled in any of the following areas:

1) A job that deals with the media
2) A job with the Catholic Church
3) A job where I can develop my writing skills

I put this in my Bible and prayed everyday that I would be allowed to work where I could use, and more fully develop, my talents and creativity. "Please guide me where you want me to be, Lord, and open the way."

I stopped looking for a job, because I knew that God would provide. A few weeks later, my friend Ei called about a job working for the Catholic Church in the Communications Office. It seems that her boss, Gonzo, had gone to the administrative center to pick up some equipment. That was the first and last time he was ever in the building, but he became the catalyst for my new job.

Eileen Marx, who was then Director of Communications, passed Gonzo in the hall. She later said she had no idea why she mentioned to him that she was looking for an assistant. He, in turn, went back to his office and mentioned it to his secretary, Ei. Almost as a joke she phoned me and said, "How would you like to write for Cardinal Hickey of the Archdiocese of Washington?" I told her I didn't think so. After all, who was I to write for a Cardinal? "No, no, I don't have enough experience," I said. I hung up the phone and went back to my work, but it kept nagging at me. I couldn't get it out of my mind until, finally, I called her back for more information.

I phoned the director, got an appointment and, within weeks, started my new job as the communications assistant. That's when I opened my Bible to read what I had placed there. I had asked for one of three things in a job: the media, the Church, or writing — to my amazement, the job was all three.

An even stranger twist is that when Eileen, the Director of Communications, first came to Washington, she called an organization where Ei was working at the time to ask if they had any openings for someone in her field. Ei told her they didn't, but suggested that she call the person who was, at that time, head of communications for the Archdiocese. Eileen was hired to represent the Cardinal as his public relations person and eventually became Director of Communications. Life is built on threads woven in a pattern that only God knows.

Just prior to getting the job in Communications, I decided to finally put into practice something I had read a few years before, but never felt I was ready to pursue. As long as I was embarking on a new adventure, it seemed a good time to better equip myself with a more positive attitude. I was re-reading a book entitled: *Power Through Constructive Thinking* by Ernest Holmes. One of the chapters, The Seven-Day Mental Diet, had fascinated me since reading it a couple of years earlier. Although I found it intriguing at the time, I had been a little afraid of putting it into action. But now I was ready.

The book stated, "Everything in life is entirely conditioned by the thoughts and feelings you choose to entertain." It further read, "Devote one week solely to building a new habit of thought and it will be a turning point for you. For seven days you must not allow yourself to dwell on any kind of negative thought. This discipline will be strenuous so you cannot maintain it for much more than a week. As soon as a negative thought presents itself, turn it out. Do not accept it. This will be exceedingly difficult for the first few days but, if you persevere, you will be amazed at the good results. A warning though — people often find that the starting of this mental diet seems to stir up all sorts of difficulties. It may seem as if everything begins to go wrong. Things will begin to move, but hold on, and when your world stops rocking, you will be the better for it."

The optimum phrase here is — *things will begin to move* ... for on the second morning of the seven-day mental diet, I walked out to the parking lot to get into my car for work and discovered it wasn't where I remembered parking it. So I walked up the street figuring I had forgotten where I had parked. When I got to the top of the hill and didn't see it, I decided to walk back down in the middle of the street, looking on both sides. By the time I got to the bottom of the hill, I knew — my car was gone. "*Things will begin to move ...* " this was true — all four tires. Having agreed to begin this experiment, I was determined not to fail simply because I had been thrown a challenge. The book also said, "Your world will be the better for it ..." So I kept the faith and remained positive. I went back into my apartment and, after giving the police a report, called for a co-worker to give me a ride to work. "What's wrong — won't your car start?"

"No," I said calmly, "it's not that. You see, I believe it's been stolen."

It took two weeks for the police to find my car. It was discovered parked at the university and had been there since the morning it was stolen. The reason the police knew it had been there since that morning was that someone whose initials were MO had placed a parking ticket on the windshield each day beginning at 5:15 on the morning it was reported missing. Now, MO wasn't too swift. The driver's side window was down, the door lock had been removed and the ignition switch dislodged. The car could only be started with a screwdriver. There were plenty of clues that this might be a stolen car, but MO never caught on. There were a total of $450 in parking tickets, which I was not responsible to pay once they realized the car had been stolen. Fortunately, the only expense was the replacement of the lock and ignition, otherwise "my world stopped rocking" and to my amazement, given the challenge, I chose to remain positive and learned the valuable lesson that a good attitude means more than the facts.

#####

Often, young people at play pretend to be someone else. They can change identities in an instant. I remember dressing up in my grandmother's clothes, or in old curtains she was ready to throw away. I could be anyone I wanted to be. I need to keep that in mind — I can be anyone I want to be — I just need to be willing to change.

Chapter 19 **Cast Your Bread Upon The Waters**

"The Wall is gone!" was the cry of the people whose lives had been challenged by the Berlin Wall. Now, souvenir rocks were being chiseled out of what was once a symbol of oppression. I, too, cried out as the walls of my own oppression continued to crumble. I went forward into the future — a new job, and faith in a God who leads the way — if only we allowed him to take the lead.

As I entered the Pastoral Center, the old compound building, once a seminary, rambled in all directions. It had an antiquated feel about it. Its long hallways, courtyard and chapel seemed to hold a myriad of memories of times gone by. I had prayed for nearly fifteen years for the chance to work for the Catholic Church and had from time to time explored job opportunities but without success. Now God had led me in his own way and in his own time. *"Cast your bread upon the waters, for you will find it after many days." (Ecclesiastes 11:1)*

My job in the Communications Office proved to be all that I had hoped for. Eileen, the director, who was an affirming person, let me know how much she valued my work and valued me as a person. Rosemarie worked only two days a week but what she gave to all of us, and the quality of her work, were welcomed gifts. Wil was hired as a twenty-hour a week employee, but soon became the assistant director, having a background ideal for the position. John, the fifth member of our team, owned his own video production company and was also the Coordinator of Radio and TV for the Archdiocese. Both Wil and John were talented men whose good humor helped to break up the tensions of the day. We were a great team and, while our office was small, it took on a dynamic quality.

I became the stabilizer, making sure everything went according to schedule and all details were accomplished. There were tight deadlines and often the day changed dramatically as news broke. I had to remain flexible to handle the creative aspects of my job, as well as constant interruptions from the media and general public as news broke about the Church. I learned to listen intently and to calm anger and fears. I had good training in those areas from working at the consultant firm.

The job was the most imaginative position I had held and I found myself richly fulfilled creatively. It was my job to type and edit the newsletter that was sent twice a month to all the parishes. I had to coordinate and oversee the mailings and there were always inserts to the newsletter from other offices, so we could have up to ten or more people participating at those mailings. I remember the first time I met with the other offices for the mailing. I had no idea what I was to tell them to do. They looked at me and I looked at them. Finally, I said, "Well, everyone has experience with these mailings, so why don't you just sit down and get started." And with that, they did!

I also worked on a publication called *Celebrate*! This was a small brochure mailed to people who were ill or unable to attend Mass, but who could participate by viewing the Mass for Shut-ins on Sunday morning TV. *Celebrate*! became an important part of my work and I loved the creativity it required of me. I was constantly searching for inspirational writings and researching passages from Scripture. I also did clip-art graphics, arranging composites to correspond with the story line.

One of my favorite duties was the simple job of the elevator bulletin board. It was one of the first impressions for people coming in from the outside and, with many offices placing items on the board, it was often in disarray. So it was decided that the Communications Office would be responsible for the bulletin board. The elevator became my job and I gave much thought to the best kinds of displays to use, other than simply putting up notices.

One day I decided that what we needed were positive messages for people to read and assimilate that might help to overcome the negatives that interject on any job. It evolved into an inspirational bulletin board. I used affirming messages and occasionally wrote something inspirational of my own, always coupled with Scripture. During holidays, I would have a running theme depicting the celebration. It was a great success. People would stop by my office to thank me for giving them these uplifting messages. They would tell me that when the day was going badly and they had a chance to use the elevator, they went back to the office feeling as if they had just heard a good sermon. In fact, some of the priests used the quotes and stories in their Sunday homilies. People from outside the building also let me know it was a pleasure to take the elevator because they were always met with something uplifting.

In my personal life, money was again becoming a challenge. My mother was now in a nursing home in Southern Maryland, a four-hour round-trip. My transportation was a seventeen-year-old car that had been given to me. With no rubber to insulate the windows, the rain seeped inside the car and very often the seat was wet. In winter, the water froze so I would wrap my legs in a blanket to keep warm. The heater and defroster were broken so, besides scraping the ice off the outside windows, I had to scrape the inside as well and, when I exhaled, the windshield iced up again. During winter, I drove with an ice scraper in hand to scrape my icy breath off the glass.

I knew the car had transmission problems but, considering its age, spending money on repairs was out of the question. I drove the four-hour roundtrip to and from the nursing home each weekend, praying the car would not die on the side of the road. I bargained with God that when the end came, if he would allow the car to die in Greenbelt, I would not complain about the drive to

Southern Maryland. It was a good bargain and when the car finally expired, I was forewarned. While backing into a parking place at the nursing home, I heard the transmission clanking loudly — a sort of death rattle. I prayed I'd get the car home and, when the end came, I was indeed only three blocks from home.

This was a much quieter demise than with my previous car. The engine in that car had caught fire while driving home one afternoon, with smoke curling out from under the hood and flames licking at my feet from the floorboard. People shouted, "Hey, lady, do you know your car's on fire?" Well, of course, I knew my car was on fire, but I was determined to get it off the street and into my own parking lot before it died. I prayed, "Lord, give me green traffic lights all the way!" I got green lights and pulled into my parking lot just before the big explosion. And so, another car was put to rest.

I enjoyed spending time at the nursing home. The nurses were fabulous and there were a lot of activities for my mother — some of the activities I could enjoy with her. My only complaint was that, although I brought her laundry home, her clothing was often missing, mostly new clothing, nightgowns and dresses which were expensive to keep replacing. By now Mama was very much like a little girl and could not understand why I couldn't simply replace the missing clothing she needed. I did the best I could and finally took on a weekend job for a few months. This meant working seven days a week without a day off. I adjusted my schedule, working Saturdays and Sundays and driving to the nursing home on Saturday evenings. By then, Mama had moved to a nursing home an hour closer, so the drive wasn't as long and, by this time, I had a better car.

One afternoon I got a phone call from the nursing home. My mother had been taken to the hospital unable to speak, or to breathe without artificial support. By the time I arrived she was in intensive care, on a respirator, with a breathing tube in her throat. They weren't certain what the problem was, but thought possibly a sensor in the back of the brain periodically shut down so the brain didn't signal to her to breathe. The doctors told me there was nothing they could do to alleviate the problem, that she would likely have to rely indefinitely on the ventilator to breathe for her.

I quit the weekend job and drove to the hospital as many evenings as I could. Mama was in the Intensive Care Unit for three and a half months, her hands tied to the sides of the bed to keep her from pulling out the breathing tube. I could tell by the look in her eyes that she didn't want to live this way. She was too much a free spirit to rely on a machine to control her life.

Each time I visited the hospital her eyes pleaded with me to do something to help her. She was determined to end her suffering and whenever her hands were free, would pull out the breathing tube, so they continued to keep her hands tied. The doctors gave me no hope for her recovery. They said it was up to me to decide if the ventilator was to be removed. I couldn't tell them to remove it because that meant certain death. Finally, the doctors suggested removing the breathing apparatus very slowly, over a period of weeks, cutting back every few days on the amount of oxygen she was given. They said this way they could tell how much she was able to breathe on her own and how much the machine had to assist her.

Right before Easter the ventilator was completely removed and she was transferred to a regular hospital room. It was a wonderful relief for her. Although she never regained her speech, she had a broad smile each time I visited. But I had a strange feeling when I saw her on Easter. She didn't want to let go of my hand and when I left that day, I could tell by the look in her eyes that she was afraid for me to go. I assured her I would be back the next evening. I suppose when someone has been so very ill thcy sense when the end is near. I believe my mother knew. "It's okay," I assured her when I left that day. "I'll be back tomorrow." But she stared at me with such an impassioned gaze; as if she knew it would be the last time she would see me. I had a haunting feeling all the way home.

The hospital called the next morning to tell me my mother had died in the early hours of the morning. She had been doing so well. For a whole week she was able to breathe on her own and seemed to be improving, but her heart was overtaxed and simply gave out. It was just like my mother to prove to the hospital staff that she could breathe without the machine. My feeling is that she was determined not to die on that machine and, right to the end, she did it her way.

At Mama's memorial Mass, I said a few words to those who had come to pay their respects. I said that my mother had not been very domesticated, that I never learned from her to cook or to clean house. But what I did learn from my mother was to be courageous. I read from a poem written by Veronica A. Shoffstall. It read:

"After a while you learn that love doesn't mean leaning, that kisses aren't contracts, and presents aren't promises. And you begin to accept defeats with your head up and your eyes open, with the grace of a woman, not the grief of a child. So you plant your own garden and decorate your own soul, instead of waiting for someone to bring you flowers. And you learn that you can endure, that you really are strong and you really do have worth, and that with every new tomorrow comes the dawn." This *was* my mother.

At work, Eileen was pregnant with her second child, Teresa. Her son, Bobby, was going to have a baby sister. It was because of this pregnancy that she and her husband, Joe, decided it was time she became a full-time mom, and it was during this time that the office structure began to change. In the midst of all the shifting, I felt a stirring inside that by now was so familiar. Something new was about to happen. I didn't know exactly what to expect, but I could feel it coming.

Within a few weeks I started my new job in the Office of the Cardinal. I could almost hear God saying, "So you want to work for the Church, do you?" For I worked long hours, but by now I was used to coordinating many things and organization came easily to me. Life in the Cardinal's Office was challenging, but my capacity for challenge had expanded with each job. I became the secretary to Cardinal Hickey's priest secretary, Father William Lori, now the Archbishop of Baltimore. Then, after he was named Chancellor of the Archdiocese, I worked as secretary to Father Barry Knestout, now an Auxiliary Bishop of Washington, who at that time became Cardinal Hickey's priest secretary. But I never got too comfortably set in my ways. Life never allows it. And before long another career change came when the Cardinal's personal assistant, Pat, retired in January 1997, and I became the Cardinal's secretary.

#####

When I was four years old, I had a cat named Fluffy. One summer, my grandparents, who were living in the Washington area, were packing to move from one side of town to another. In all the commotion, Fluffy got lost and though we hunted for her for two days, she was not to be found. So my grandparents had no alternative but to move from where we were living into our new home, without Fluffy. I was heart broken.

Days later, while we were getting settled in the new house, I heard a very loud "meow" at the front door. When I went to investigate, there was Fluffy — dirty, hungry, but happy to have found her new home. I was amazed! We hugged and I vowed not to let her out of my sight ever again. It was a good lesson for me about faith and perseverance. Fluffy had cast her bread upon the waters and after many days of wandering, found her heart's desire. What a faithful spirit.

Chapter 20 **Life Is Change**

I have always loved to write. When I was twelve, after seeing *Gone With the Wind* for the first time, I was inspired to write a novel called *New Dawn in My Castle.* It was quite lofty and written from the maturity level of a twelve-year-old, but it was a disciplined effort. In my teens I wrote poetry, short stories, and music lyrics. So, as an adult, writing seemed a natural development for me.

I began writing seriously in the late `90s and by 1996, after completing several manuscripts, began sending them to publishing houses. I began to receive rejections to my submissions, but I had worked hard to believe in my abilities, and in myself, and was not going to allow those letters to dictate my worth as a writer. In my heart I knew I had to write. It was part of that destiny I had been pursuing for so many years.

I stormed heaven quite a lot, asking God to direct me toward the right publishers for my work. I also prayed my favorite novena to Saint Therese. Then one weekend I attended a lecture series on Saint Therese, prior to her being named Doctor of the Church. During the lecture, her poetry was read. I was most impressed with her poem entitled, *The Unpetalled Rose*. It deeply touched me, especially that of her soul remaining unadorned so that nothing would come between herself and God when she prayed.

The following day, during the celebration of Mass, I asked Saint Therese for a rose — a rose where all the petals had fallen off — an unpetalled rose. I wanted it as a reminder to always keep my spirit childlike and unencumbered. After Mass, the congregation was invited to the altar to receive a red rose. As we moved forward, each person received a beautiful rose from the armful the presiding priest held. When it was my turn, the priest pulled a rose from the cluster and handed it to me. It was a simple stem with leaves — all the petals had fallen off. Out of nearly 200 people, I was the only one to receive an "unpetalled rose."

Just as astounding to me, while I sat in one of the lectures, out of nowhere came the idea for a book. It seemed to run right through my head like rushing wind. I thought about it and decided that I was being directed to write a book of prayers. I began writing about my conversations with God and sending out proposals. Then, one day the phone rang. It was Honor Books. They were interested in publishing my book to be titled, *Uncommon Conversations With God,* published under Honor Books' new imprint, River Oak Publishing. After all the prayers and my belief in the answers to those prayers, my dream was coming true. *If you have faith like a mustard seed, you will say to this mountain, remove from here and it will remove. And nothing will be impossible to you. — Matthew 17:20.*

Life is change, and change is an adventure into the unknown. Without trust in God, those adventures can rock our security and throw us into panic. By keeping hope alive and developing a keen interest in, and an acceptance of, the "unknown," we cooperate with God's plan — *"For with God all things are possible." Matthew 19:26.*

While on the subject of the unknown, I would like to say a few words regarding angels. I have always believed in angels, but until I experienced a particular incident, angels were something lofty; heavenly creatures depicted on greeting cards but not actually part of my reality. However, one day that changed in an instant and when it did, I began to wonder if the times I have felt touched by God were indeed acts carried out by his angels.

I was to attend a social celebration for a dear friend, and though I looked forward to going, it was difficult because of the time constraints I was under at work that week. By the time I left work that Friday, I had worked nearly 60 hours, and in order to leave that day by 3:30, I was in the office by 7:00 a.m. I had worked three late evenings in a row and when I picked up my friend, Ei, and were on our way, it was a real struggle for me to stay alert.

When we arrived, realizing that the neighborhood was not the safest, I secured my car with a steel lock-up bar, a device suggested previously by the police when my car had been stolen — a bar that wrapped around the brake and steering column and locked with a key. I had always wondered what would happen if someone tried to drive my car with this bar in place. That evening I found out.

It was an enjoyable evening but by 11:00 p.m. I could barely hold up. After another half-hour on the parking lot saying goodbye to friends, we headed for my car to make the trip to Ei's and then home. But in my haste to get on the road, it never occurred to me to remove the lock-up bar. In fact, I was so tired that I hadn't remembered using the bar and, because there were no streetlights, I never noticed it when I got in the car.

I started the engine, pressed down on the accelerator and pulled out of the parking space. I didn't get very far. Suddenly I realized I had no control over my car. I couldn't move the steering wheel, nor could I operate the brake. However, the car continued to move forward in a circular motion. No sooner had I pulled out of the parking spot than my car began to circle left, heading for the eight cars parked in a row on the lot. It all happened so quickly that I had no time to discern the problem. I yelled, "I've lost control of the car! Just hold on!" And indeed, that's all we could do at that second. Then my car, as if moving in slow motion, maneuvered past the parked vehicles, circled left again, around the last car, then glided left toward an available open space, a space just vacated by the people who had left ahead of us. My car maneuvered through the parking space, and with cars on both sides, came out clean without touching either parked car. It was then that I realized the bar was in place, turned off the ignition and yanked up the emergency brake.

Ei and I were both so shaken by the experience that we laughed hysterically. When I think of the damage I could have caused, I shudder. I could see the headlines — Cardinal's secretary demolishes eight cars belonging to local priests. What a disaster that could have been. I know in my heart that God had sent his angels to help. Ei said she had never experienced anything like it. I continue to get cold chills at the thought of it — my car, out of control, moving as if on air. *"For He will command His angels concerning you to guard you in all your ways." Psalms 91:11.*

#####

When I was young, the 5 & 10-cent stores sold turtles about the size of a quarter. I remember picking out a tiny turtle and buying a small glass bowl for his home. It didn't take long to come up with an appropriate name for my turtle. For such a small creature, he was very strong so I decided to name him Samson, but Samson was not only strong, he was smart. I had filled his bowl with smooth flat rocks so he would have places to hide and to sleep, but Samson found another use for them. Every day he would push the rocks with his head until he had piled them as high as they would go, then he would climb up to the top of the pile, trying to escape.

Once I saw what he had done, I would place the rocks back where they had been. But Samson never gave up. He would spend most of his day moving those rocks. One day he finally succeeded. When I went to feed him, Samson was nowhere to be found.

I often wondered where he had gone in search of his adventures, but I never found the answer. That tiny turtle, no bigger than a coin, believed that all things were possible and when he encountered a mountain, simply learned to climb it. Thanks, Samson, for the faith-filled lesson. I have often thought about your tenacity and your vision.

Chapter 21 **The Cardinal's Good Humor**

I worked for the Archdiocese of Washington for fifteen years, the first year and a half as an assistant to Eileen Marx, Communications Director in the Office of Communications. After that I transferred to the Cardinal's Office as secretary to then-Father William Lori, the cardinal's priest secretary. Father Lori was later named chancellor and then Auxiliary Bishop of Washington. He was later appointed Bishop of Bridgeport in Connecticut. He has since been installed as Archbishop of Baltimore. Msgr. Barry Knestout followed as secretary to Cardinal Hickey, and I became the monsignor's secretary. He has since been elevated to Auxiliary Bishop of Washington. As I mentioned before, in 1997, when the cardinal's long-time personal assistant, Pat Wright, retired, I was fortunate enough to work directly for Cardinal Hickey as his secretary.

While working in the Cardinal's Office, my friends and colleagues helped me on my journey by gifting me with their kindness and their humor, and I have made it part of who I am. Both Archbishop Lori and Bishop Knestout gave the gifts of themselves. Again, I learned many things during these years. The work was not always easy, and I had to stretch my mind to keep up with the tasks, but I felt good when given the opportunity to see what I was capable of accomplishing, and to have such confidence placed in me. During those years, my belief in myself and in my abilities rose to a new level of self-worth. When the people we admire believe in us, it changes how we see ourselves.

Cardinal Hickey was a gracious, kind man whose sense of humor gave me much joy. While working in the cardinal's first floor office, but not yet as his secretary, I connected with his wonderful sense of humor. I had been working on the Christmas thank you letters and, as usual, the phone was constantly ringing, interrupting my progress. For much of the correspondence I used a form letter, changing the wording to fit the gift. I had been typing thank you letters for flowers sent to the cardinal, but had just started a letter thanking the person for a delicious ham. I was changing the message when the phone rang. Once I took care of the caller, I went back to the computer, finished the letter and printed it on letterhead. That's when I read what I had typed. The letter read:

> I write to thank you for the thoughtful gift of the smoked ham, which you sent to me for Christmas. The ham added much joy to my celebration of Christmas. (Here the phone rang, then I continued with), I have placed it in the chapel of my residence where its presence will enhance the beauty of the sanctuary while I celebrate Mass during the Christmas season.

I was laughing at my mistake when the cardinal came through the office from a meeting he had attended in the adjacent room. He asked what I was laughing about, so I showed him the letter. Between spontaneous laughter he said, "That's the best typo I've ever read." It truly became his favorite. I can still hear him laughing out loud as he disappeared down the hall.

And I loved the stories he would tell about his younger days as a priest. One such story was about his first trip to Rome. As a young priest, gathering experiences for his long tenure, Father Hickey had his share of awkward moments. He recounts his trip to Rome: "The year was 1959. I was still serving as secretary to Bishop Stephen Woznicki of Saginaw, my home diocese. We were making the required five-year visit to Rome and had an appointment to see Pope John XXIII who, at that time, was staying at the summer papal villa at Castel Gandolfo, outside Rome.

Bishop Woznicki was invited to visit privately with the Holy Father. After Pope John and my bishop had conversed for a time, I was ushered into the room.

"When I entered, their backs were turned as they were looking out the window at the beautiful view of the lake. Nevertheless, I thought I should observe the already fading protocol of genuflecting three times as I approached the pope. I must admit I felt foolish genuflecting to the pope when he wasn't even looking my way! Nonetheless, the first genuflection went smoothly enough. By the second genuflection, I was flustered. At the third genuflection, very near where Pope John and my bishop were standing, I got all tangled up in my clerical attire — especially the ample floor-length cape that used to be *de rigueur* for papal audiences. So when Pope John and my bishop turned around, I was on all fours! My dear bishop greeted the sight with astonishment. Quite understandably, he couldn't imagine what I was doing on the floor! Fortunately, Pope John smiled, helped me up and dusted me off. 'I was once a bishop's secretary,' he whispered, 'I understand!'"

I have come to believe that prayer is a two-way conversation with God. God knows us totally and is not surprised by anything we tell him. What we call intuition, or instinct, is really that small voice inside where God speaks to us, if we open our spirits to hear him. I experienced God's voice while working for the Archdiocese when I was warned of impending danger, even before I knew danger was about to cross my path.

I was preparing to close the office at the end of the workday. Closing time was 5:00 pm, and I never left the office before 5:00. But that day I had a feeling I couldn't explain, a feeling urging me to leave work early. At first, I dismissed it. It didn't make sense, as there was no reason to leave early. But by ten minutes to 5:00 I could no longer ignore the urgency I felt. I quickly locked up the office and headed for my car, feeling a little foolish for giving in to my urge.

As it turned out, that urge was a direct prompt that may have saved my life. Driving by the University of Maryland that afternoon, I had reason to be grateful that I hadn't disregarded that small voice. There was a warning on my car radio that a tornado was about to touch down at Maryland University at 5:22. I glanced at the clock. It was 5:22. In my rearview mirror, I saw a funnel cloud quickly approaching. It looked dark and ominous as it rotated toward me. I pushed hard on the car's accelerator in an attempt to outrun it, aware that had I left work at 5:00, my usual time, I would have been caught up in the funnel cloud. Because I listened to that small voice inside, I was able to make it to safety. Later in the week, I drove to the area where the tornado had touched down. The destruction was devastating. Having had that experience, I always listen to God's voice, even though it may not come as an audible expression, speaking to me in words, but more likely a feeling deep inside, urging me with a sense of guidance.

#####

While in kindergarten, I invited my entire class home after school for my birthday party, only my grandmother didn't know I was bringing the children home and hadn't planned a party. Many of the children couldn't come, but the ones who lived nearby did. When my grandmother saw us and I told her they were there to celebrate my birthday party, she lined us up and walked us to the nearest High's ice cream store where she bought each of us a huge ice cream cone. I guess it wasn't funny at the time, but when I think of it now, I can't help but laugh.

Chapter 22 **Serendipities**

While working in the Cardinal's office, I was given a very touching experience of love one evening when I was privileged to meet Mother Teresa. I had been working on a talk that she was to give and, with four thousand copies to be printed, the deadline seemed impossible. I struggled to bring the job to completion on time and when the people came to pick up the talk it was after 6:00 p.m.

I walked out to the van to open the door for the driver as he placed the boxes inside. As I did, I glanced up and was astonished to see Mother Teresa sitting on the passenger side of the van. I could tell by her expression that she knew I had been the one who had prepared her talk. Twice she tried to find the handle to open the car window but couldn't since, I'm sure, it was automatic. Finally, in her loving spirit, she did what she could to make contact with me. She gently pressed her hand against the windowpane, spreading her fingers over the glass for me to cover her hand with my own. Even through the cold glass, I could feel the warmth of her love as her tender gaze met mine in the twilight. It was a silent, very intimate moment of communication that I shall never forget. A few moments before, I had been feeling the stress of my afternoon task. Now, all the tension and strain had melted away. For in that moment, I was allowed to see Christ living in Mother Teresa and the impact of that brief encounter touched my spirit. I discovered in that special moment the enormous power of love and the mighty strength of simplicity.

Another serendipity of working in the Cardinal's office came one afternoon when I got a call from a man named Willis, who said he was in town traveling with Rosa Parks, the Mother of the Modern Day Civil Rights Movement. They had read where Pope John Paul II had made a rare trip to the U.S. and was in St. Louis.

"Mrs. Parks," he said, "would like to meet the Pope. Could that be arranged?"

It took me a minute to recover from the shock. It was short notice, but I thought, if Rosa Parks wants to meet the Pope, then she should. Cardinal Hickey and the Bishops were already on their way to St. Louis. I knew I had to depend on whatever resources I could find to arrange such a meeting. I made a few calls to no avail. Then I called a bishop who was involved in the event in St. Louis and asked the name of the appropriate person to reach with the power to make a decision. Once I was able to reach that person, a meeting was scheduled between these two very extraordinary people. But that was not the end of it for me.

I found Elaine, a friend who was as close to Mrs. Parks as a daughter, and Willis, who advanced for Mrs. Parks, to be gracious people. When they returned to Washington from St. Louis, they not only invited me to meet with them in appreciation of my efforts, but also invited me to attend Mrs. Parks' 86th birthday celebration as well — a great honor. Then, before leaving town, they again invited me to a private breakfast with the three of them.

It was a rare privilege to meet the legendary Rose Parks, who would not relinquish her seat to a white male passenger on the orders of a bus driver in 1955, sparking the Civil Rights Movement. Mrs. Parks, who was serene with a healing demeanor, blessed others with her calming presence and through her gentle touch. Meeting Rosa Parks and spending time with these three extraordinary people will remain one of my fondest memories.

It is always such a pleasure when God sends us special gifts that we weren't expecting. In his own timing, he plans our surprises, and there we are, face-to-face with a special serendipity we would never have dreamed of. I have come to believe that God sends us many such surprises, but we don't always realize it when it's happening. Once we learn to recognize them, he will delight in sending us even more.

Both Mother Teresa and Rosa Parks shared their love. It was an extraordinary opportunity to have had the privilege of interacting with them. They are part of my special memories.

#####

As a child, I remember reading the wonderful story of The Velveteen Rabbit by Margery Williams. She wrote: “Real isn’t how you are made,” said the Skin Horse. “It’s a thing that happens to you ... When a child loves you for a long, long time, not just to play with, but really loves you, then you become Real …”

When I read her story, I thought, *I hope I will be loved like that.* And as I look back on my life, I realize that so many people have contributed to my becoming *Real.*

Chapter 23 **<u>My Lucky Break</u>**

By the late 90s, I began to wonder about my retirement years. I had been in my apartment for over twenty-five years, but knew, with the yearly rental increases, that the rent on the apartment would not be affordable living on a fixed retirement income.

That's when the idea of buying a house first beckoned. To buy a freestanding house with a low down payment meant that, once retired, I could not afford the house payment. To buy one of the Greenbelt Cooperative Homes in my neighborhood, though the house payment would be affordable, I would need 10% of the purchase price up front as a down payment. How could I come up with that kind of money? Still, my dream of having my own place would not leave me alone. I began to pray about it, asking God to help me find a way to buy a house before I was priced out of my apartment.

Before long I found myself bringing home boxes from the grocery store to pack up some of my belongings. What began with packing things I hardly used, became a full-fledged attempt to learn to live with only my bare essentials. I had no idea where I might move and had no means of financing a move. Still, I couldn't shake the compulsion to pack up everything in my apartment. I thought to myself, *All I did was ask God for help and now I can't stop packing everything in sight.* This went on for months until I had boxes climbing to the ceiling in my bedroom. Someone asked if I were planning to move. I remember telling them that I was. When they asked where I was going, I said I didn't know, but I am obviously going somewhere!

I continued to pray, this time asking God for a *lucky break*. Having written a couple of books, I figured that if I could find an interested publisher, I might make some extra money to save toward my house. I prayed for months for a *lucky break.* At the time, I was working for Cardinal Hickey and helping to plan the Convocation for the Archdiocese of Washington. It was to be a huge gathering of people at the Convention Center. I was one of the main planners. I was asked to spend the night at the hotel across the street from the Convention Center so I could start work the next morning by 6:00.

I awoke at 5:00 a.m. and headed to the shower. I did all the correct things — placing the towel mat on the floor ahead of time, drying off before stepping out of the tub, making sure I stepped out safely. All went well as I lifted my left leg out of the tub after my shower. But something went terribly wrong as I lifted my right leg over the side. The tiled floor was extremely slick and I suddenly felt the tub mat flying backwards like a magic carpet. My foot found the one small space between the wall and cabinet that enabled my fall, otherwise, had my foot gone in any other direction, it would have blocked my fall. So, there I was, somewhere in space, flying on my *magic carpet.*

The next thing I knew, I fell from *space* and landed on my right arm on the tiled floor. I was stunned. I wasn't sure what had just happened, but I knew I had to pick myself up off the floor and get to the phone. I positioned my left hand to raise myself up, but I couldn't find my right hand. That's when I realized that my right arm was in back of me. I pulled up on the sink with my left hand, reaching around to locate my right arm and pulling it to the front. However, anticipating a modest appearance as the hotel people came into the room, I let go of my arm to reach for a towel. My arm swung around in back of me again. This time, I pulled my arm around and held it securely against the sink while I wrapped the towel around me with my left hand. Somehow, I made it to the phone and called the front desk before my body crumpled. As I attempted to walk toward the door of my room, my body went into shock and I slid to the floor — still holding my arm against my side. I was sitting at the foot of the bed, bracing my arm against the mattress when the people from the hotel came into the room, followed by two paramedics. At the hospital they told me I had broken my upper arm in three places but it was too severe for them to perform emergency surgery. They said to see an orthopedic surgeon. I thought, *I did pray for a lucky break.*

I found an orthopedic doctor in the phone book. As it turned out, he was an older man who believed in conservative treatments. He said most doctors would probably have operated, placing a steel plate in my upper arm but, had he done this, it would have rendered only partial use of my arm. Instead, he asked if I would trust him to take the conservative route. I said I would, so he placed me in a hanging cast. This meant that for nearly five months I could do nothing but sit on my couch, supported by pillows, with my arm bent so that my hand was up toward my shoulder and my elbow hanging toward the floor. If I moved my arm too much the bones rubbed together, causing pain. So I sat erect day and night. I couldn't take a shower or even lean over the sink for someone to wash my hair.

However, the doctor's idea was working, and gravity gradually pulled the broken bones together. When the bones were as close as they could get, I watched each week as the X-ray showed calcium from my body filling in the open spaces between the bones. It was like watching an arm being built and was unforgettable. With physical therapy, my arm healed perfectly.

During this time of healing, I received a phone call from the hotel. They wanted to offer me a settlement for my accident. It seemed it really had been a *lucky break.* (God's plans are not always our plans.) I did ask God why I couldn't have simply won the lottery — and I haven't asked for a *lucky break* since!

Those five months were a time of healing in many ways. For

the first time in years, I had the opportunity to find peace inside with God as my constant companion, and now I had the down payment needed for a house. It was amazing.

Now, while I don't suggest a person sustain a broken arm as a means of having prayers answered, it certainly seems that my *lucky break* was a direct answer to my prayers (be careful what you ask for). Somehow, with all the suffering and turmoil, peace and contentment filled my life to overflowing. It's so true that God often brings blessings from turbulence. Life is frequently like that for me — there is much chaos, then God uses that earthly turmoil to reconstruct my life, bringing with it heavenly blessings — another of life's mysteries. Of course, I often go along protesting — but God knows me and he's not a bit surprised.

Because of my *lucky break*, I had enough down payment for my Greenbelt Cooperative home. Once the settlement came from the hotel, I started looking at homes. However, none of the advertised homes for sale really appealed to me. Then, as I was driving home, my eye caught a for sale sign in the yard of a home not posted on the list of homes for sale. This house was for sale by the owner. I parked my car to look at the house more closely. From the outside it seemed perfect, so I called for someone to open up the house so I could see the inside. The house was just as perfect inside as it was outside. It had a third bedroom that I could use for an office, and bathrooms on both floors. And the view from the back of the house overlooked a wooded area. I loved it. The house was mine, even if I did have to break my arm to buy it!

#####

When I was growing up, people would say, "be careful what you ask for." I never understood what they meant. Lying on that hotel bathroom floor, I finally knew what they had been talking about. But God took care of the whole thing, and I now had my lovely home.

Chapter 24 **Signs of Hope**

Several years ago, my son, Joe, established his own paint business, but realized when the economy began to plunge and home owners were cutting back on home improvements, that he was bringing in less money than he paid in expenses. He put his resume in for a job at one of the local universities and waited five long months.

One weekend in late summer, I drove to Delaware with my friend Lee to visit our friends, Joan and John. While there, we went to one of the casinos. I am not much of a gambler, so I decided to play the penny machine. Even though I won a few cents along the way, I was getting bored with gambling. So I decided to pray while sitting there, talking to God about Joe's need for the job he had applied for.

I asked God to send me a sign so I would know that Joe would be hired. I was feeling quite desperate and in need of hope. I said to God, "As long as I'm gambling, if three consecutive numbers come up on this machine, I will consider it a sign that Joe will be hired."

I played the penny machine until I got down to my last five cents, each time pulling the lever, and waiting for the numbers to come up. The machine went from five cents to four, then three, then two, and on my very last penny I watched as 777 came up. That was my sign. Two days later, Joe got a call from the university telling him he was hired, and two days after that, the university put a freeze on hiring for the next two years.

A few days later, I was driving into D.C. to a location I was not familiar with. I was really afraid of getting lost and not getting there on time. Traffic in D.C. is always a problem. I stopped at a gas station to top off my gas so I would at least have a full tank. While waiting for the gas to stop pumping, I again prayed to God that he would get me there safely and on time. As I pulled off my receipt, I glanced at the total. It was $7.77. I had to smile. God has a sense of humor. "Thank you," I whispered, knowing everything would be just fine — and it was.

I have always asked God for signs when I'm in need of hope. I had been going through some personal dark times that seemed to have no solutions, no answers. It was disheartening. God knew the answers, but He had yet to reveal them to me. So I continue to wait for God to direct me toward solutions to my challenges.

During dark times, I cry out to God that I am in desperate need of a sign from him to know he is working on those impasses. He often gives me messages of hope to sustain me while I wait for answers.

A few years later, after Joe's wife had left him, I was driving home on a day that was particularly stressful. Joe's house was about to go into foreclosure. It was one of those moments when you feel you can't process any more tribulations. I prayed for a sign of hope. At a red light, an SUV pulled up beside me. I looked over and on the side window the driver had taped a sign. The sign read: NO MATTER WHAT, TRUST GOD

Often, while I wait for answers to prayers, I recalled those words — *No matter what, trust God.* They sustain me, as I wait on the Lord. In Proverbs 3:5-6 — we read: *Trust in the Lord with all your heart ... In all your ways acknowledge him, and he will make straight your paths.*

There are so many trials in life that we sometimes wonder if God will ever free us from our troubles. God's love is boundless and he has a plan for our lives — as I've experienced many times. God's plan is often revealed as he directs my path through life.

But there are times when we simply cannot comprehend where God is leading us. For that reason, he places faith within our souls.

When all reasoning fails, we live by faith, and why not — after all, until God reveals his plans to us, we have nothing to grasp other than faith in his promises, and in his guidance. Faith is our gift *from* God. Opening our spirits to his wisdom is our gift *to* God. Life is precarious, but we can be certain our Creator *is* in charge. When we storm heaven, we only win the battle if God wills it. We are in his hands all through life.

The good news is — he loves us with such a miraculous love that he listens to our pleas and, if those prayers lead us to him and not away from him, he fulfills our needs and puts hope in our hearts. We must *trust God, no matter what.* There are no other paths that lead to salvation.

Even at the end of life, when we face the unknown, we have nothing to fear. As God carries us to his heavenly home, the *extraordinary miracle* is that we are born anew in the warmth of springtime as he enfolds us in his boundless loving arms.

#####

If we become lost in the dark side of love, we need to let go and let God guide us. He will use our song of love's eclipse to change us and take us in a new direction. *God is Love*, so when we can't see diamonds dancing across the water, God will pluck the stars from the sky to fill the jar of life. If flowering petals die as the earth cools, he will send a cushion of winter snow. We are made in the image of *Love.* Life is ever evolving, taking us with it. Love is never lost — it just goes forward. As we open our spirits to the *Light* … we become *Light* — and God will teach us a new love song.

Chapter 25 **Healing Trip**

In 1990, my children and I took an extraordinary trip as a family that helped redefine our scattered relationships with one another. Joe and Debralee, who were living in California, traveled east for the vacation. Neither John nor Joe were married at the time. Two of Kathy's children, Gina and Seth, went with us. Jessica, her oldest daughter, was working out of town for the summer to make money for her next college semester and couldn't join us.

We first traveled to West Virginia for four days to stay at a cabin owned by friends, Walt and Betty. It's a restful place, set on a wooded hill overlooking the river. Just the kind of place where nature can heal and bring peace to the heart. Now that I look back on this, the trip to the West Virginia cabin was a preparation for our experience of returning to our roots, an experience that gave each of us a sense of belonging — a feeling of connecting with our heritage and with each other.

After a restful four days at the cabin, we headed to Virginia where my mother had grown up and where my maternal grandfather and his father before him had lived and died. My Aunt Joyce, my mother's sister, and her husband Gary, still live in the house where my mother was raised. We spent the day with them and decided to take a ride to the property that had once been the plantation of my great-grandfather, Samuel Davis. My mother had told me so many stories over the years of the long hallways and porches in the homestead and how she and Samuel had gone fishing along the banks of the Shenandoah River, bordering the property. I also knew that somewhere on that vast piece of land was the simple, small cemetery where many family members are buried, including my grandfather Benjamin and my great-grandfather Samuel.

My aunt knew the area and where the property was located, but she didn't know the location of the cemetery on the property. So when we arrived, we each took a different direction and combed the area for a couple of hours. Disappointed and tired from walking through the tall grass, we were unable to locate the tiny cemetery. When we met back at the location where we began our search, we came to a tall railroad bridge where the train had carried my grandfather on his daily excursion, that same bridge where he lost his life at the age of twenty. It was an eerie feeling for us to look up at that bridge with its tall steel girders and picture Benjamin as he must have looked in those days — tall, proud, soon to be a father. We stood in silence gathering our private thoughts and then Joe and John began to climb the girders to get a view from higher up where the trains travel. Each of us took home some memento from the spot. However, the cemetery had eluded us, so we headed back toward the cars a bit discouraged. Sometimes in life God gives us one of his special blessings — that magical time when everything falls into place without having to do anything — you are simply in the right place at the right time. For us, this was one of those times.

As we were backing the vehicles out of the dirt road toward the highway, I noticed a small pathway leading up a hill, which was covered with trees and overgrowth. I yelled, "Stop the cars!" We got out and started up the path. My heart was pounding. At the top of the hill, a shaft of light illuminated the path where, to our surprise and delight, though grown over with weeds, we had found the tiny cemetery. Most of the tombstones were very old and revealed no sign of who might be buried there, but off to the left we saw two large stones, one with the name Benjamin Davis and the other Samuel Davis — my grandfather and great-grandfather — the beloved Samuel whom my mother adored during her childhood, who took her fishing and taught her about life and love.

At sixteen he had written to his mother while fighting in the Civil War; a letter I still have. And I had heard the story of Sudie and Benjamin all my life, but to actually see the tombstone — to see that he had only been twenty years old when killed — that he died in July and my mother was not born until October — made it such a reality. This was really going back to our roots and all of us had our own solitary thoughts as we stood there at the gravesite; thoughts of bygone lives from which we came and from which our future heirs will be part of. It created a deep feeling of belonging to the past, and to each other.

As if this weren't enough, on the way back down the path, I noticed what was left of a chimney amidst the tall grass that had engulfed it for many years. I ran shouting that this was part of the homestead — we had found Samuel's house. All that was left was the chimney and the stone cellar, but what a thrill to actually stand were they had stood — to see the river where they had fished and where in late summer Samuel would fill his wooden raft with fruits and vegetables and head down the river to give them away to those less fortunate.

This trip brought us together in a solid, steadfast way as nothing else could have done. Whatever life holds for each of us, this memory will be part of who we are as individuals and as a family.

#####

From what *Power* do our valuable interventions come? Are they random? Hardly, for they come at such a perfect time, and in such a perfect way. It's similar to crossing a powerful stream of water. We must wade through to the other side, but our feet keep slipping in the polluted mire. Our task seems impossible — but our foot finds a stepping stone, and then another, as we are guided across the raging waters. Your timing is perfect, Lord, and your love enduring, as you scatter before us the stepping stones of life.

Chapter 26 **The Cardinal's Health Challenges**

Cardinal Hickey retired from the Archdiocese of Washington in 2000, following his 80th birthday. For the first two years following his retirement, the cardinal gave his time wherever it was needed, concelebrating Masses, giving an invocation or a short talk on occasion, attending religious professions, and traveling to newly appointed bishops' installations. But poor health and failing eyesight began to interfere with his plans. Slowly, it debilitated him more and more, until he was forced to limit many activities and travel was no longer possible.

I stayed on with the Cardinal even after he retired. He maintained an office in the Pastoral Center and I continued as his secretary. When I first noticed that health problems were ebbing away at the cardinal's strength, I felt sorrow — for the cardinal and for the Church, for he had offered his life so that God's message would remain pure and sacred.

It was then that I realized His Eminence was continuing to live out God's message. I was simply looking at that message with human eyes and not through the eyes of God. Cardinal Hickey, through his suffering, was continuing to teach us about life. He was living out the Cross of Jesus right before us. He was showing us that life is more than success, more than joyous events, more than participation in the celebrations of our human existence — life is also about the mystery of sorrow. By witnessing his difficulties, we saw that all life has meaning.

James Cardinal Hickey died on Sunday, October 24, 2004, with friends and relatives at his bedside. He died as he had lived: a peace-filled priest and beloved friend.

In a homily given at the Vigil Mass on the evening of October 29th in the Crypt Church of the Basilica, then-Bishop William Lori said of the cardinal, "These past few years have been difficult for

Cardinal Hickey. All his life he was a hard worker, an organizer, an avid reader, an effective communicator, a doer. The ravages of time and illness robbed him of all that. As his powers of speech diminished, he looked at me once very intently, squeezed my hand and said, `It's so tough. I can't say what I want to say.'

It was hard to see this happening to the cardinal and harder still for him to undergo it, but it was the Cross in a new and poignant form — a time of suffering and purification as he prepared to journey to that new and eternal Jerusalem where tears are shed no longer, where death gives way to life, where sadness surrenders to joy."

I retired from the Archdiocese of Washington in 2004 and spend a good deal of my time writing and involved with my family and friends. As I closed my office door for the last time, looking back at the dimly lit room and the Cardinal's library shelves barren of his cherished books, I realized I had experienced the end of an era.

My children are grown now with lives of their own. Debralee and her husband, David, now live in Asheville, North Carolina. Debralee has produced two videos that have received acclaim; an introduction to ballet, and a children's Mother Goose tape. She is working on a cook book, and is also an accomplished dancer and teaches ballet in Asheville.

Kathy has gone through a divorce and struggled with many of the same issues that I have, but she pushed forward with her life. She graduated from Maryland University in May 1999, after attending night classes for eight years while working a full-time job and, for many years, holding down a part-time job as well to support her children. She went on to do her graduate work for her Master's degree at George Washington University in the field she loves — American History.

John has also been divorced, but now has Donna in his life, a friend of ten years. He is a responsible dad to his son, Shaun, and works full-time as an accomplished firefighter. John has many talents and can build and repair just about anything. John and I have worked through most of our issues from the past, although I still carry the pain from those wounds inside me, as he does as well.

Joe is also divorced with children — Becky, Shayne, and Noah, and a son, Joey, living in California with his wife, Anna, and their two children. Joe started a successful paint business, but when the economy began to fail, he had to look for permanent employment, but still takes on jobs with his paint company. Joe is a gifted musician who excels in writing original music and is a talented drummer.

I take delight in my grandchildren, Jessie, Gina, Seth, Joey, Shaun, Becky, Shayne and Noah. My oldest granddaughter, Jessie, and husband, Chris, are parents of three boys. Gina is married to Walter, and they have two boys, and Seth is the father of three boys.

As we become older, our perspective expands to appreciate the delights of the world as seen through the eyes of the young, and we understand more fully the impact we have on them. As an old Chinese proverb tells us: "A child is like a blank piece of paper on which everyone who passes by writes something."

God continues to give me small miracles in my life. Life is intertwined with so many guiding miracles. When God created us, he placed a defining voice within our souls. Through this power, he guides us — if we recognize his message.

I was on my way to a funeral home one evening for the viewing of a dear friend. It was a distance and I was driving in rush-hour traffic. I drove for some time, but didn't see the funeral home, so I turned down a side street and asked a woman for directions. She told me, with much confidence, that the funeral home was in the opposite direction. I turned my car around and headed the other way.

Now it was getting late. I had twenty-five minutes, as the viewing closed at 8:00 p.m. I began to pray in earnest. I knew I couldn't attend the funeral Mass the next day. I had two scheduled medical appointments for pre-op exams, and my surgery was fast approaching.

As I prayed, I had an inner feeling that I was headed the wrong way. Listening to that urge — I would ask for directions again. I noticed a man sitting on a bench. I knew it was nearly impossible to pull over and stop my car in the heavy traffic. But as I approached the man, I noticed a curved cut-out in the sidewalk, right in front of where the man was sitting, and it was just large enough for my car to pull out of the lane of traffic.

The man walked over to my car window. He *just happened* to have a GPS on his cell phone. He told me I was driving in the wrong direction and was able to tell me the cross streets I would pass, along with the name of the cross street right before I was to turn into the parking lot. I was so grateful to that man for his help but most of all I was grateful for God's guidance. I had only fifteen minutes before the viewing closed, but it was enough time to say a prayer for my friend as I knelt beside his casket, and to speak with his family.

#####

We shall all die, but thankfully, regardless of our sinful ways, Jesus doesn't give up on us. I am certain that when we see his radiant smile and feel the warmth as he takes our hand in his, we will say, "Lord, I was hoping you'd be here to help me. You see, I want to go home. I wasn't fully aware before, but there is something missing in my soul."

And the Lord will smile and say, "I've been waiting for you. I have so many plans. I'm going to teach you to love yourself again."

Chapter 27 **The Greatest of These Is Love**

Love is what gives life its substance. Without love we may go through the motions of living out our lives, but it is a poor substitute for the kind of living that true love inspires. Often we substitute power and control for love. It seems everyone wants to be God. The bittersweet of life is that sometimes love is painful. Only God can truly heal a broken heart and only God can teach us how to mirror him in our loving.

Just as we need to embrace love, we need to embrace our solitude, for it's in solitude that we build the bridges that carry us forward to life. When we build enough bridges to continue our walk, we become free to allow our love to flow like the gentle waters of a river. *Out of the believing heart shall flow rivers of living water. John 7:38.* Life is often understood more fully in retrospect. In looking back, we find it's not the struggles that have shaped our spirits as much as the wisdom we take from those experiences to nurture souls. I watched as Nelson Mandela was released after spending twenty-seven years in captivity. He emerged to be elected to the African presidency.

That he had overcome his struggles against all odds gave me hope. He had used those painful years to grow in wisdom and used that wisdom to nurture souls. How could I do less?

Relationships are often difficult to maintain. People change; sometimes they grow in different directions, or become disillusioned with each other's differences. Relationships require work and a sensitivity to each other's needs. Real love sees the person realistically, but with a sense of their infinite dignity.

As I write this, spring is exploding before my eyes. It's as if God has run through the woods and fields shouting out his joy and awakening all of nature by the gentle touch of his hand. Love is like the springtime, full of the promises of new life. Love is a natural process that starts from within, and its potential for growth is endless. It is a life force, and to allow it to grow, we need to open our spirits and let it go free.

Jim Rosemergy wrote this about releasing love: "Years ago, infants in orphanages were dying at an alarming rate. Eventually, the infants were picked up, talked to, and cuddled often. The premise was that the children needed love to live. This need for love seems to be a denial of our way of life, for we are spiritual beings, whole and complete. Nothing needs to be added to us. However, love must be released. Spiritual insights reveal that the children lived not because they were loved, but because they were given the opportunity *to* love. In this way, love was released from within them.

"The little ones usually have a favorite stuffed animal. When the child is unhappy, the animal is hugged. In the hugging, the child feels better. Why? Was it because the teddy bear loved the child? No, the stuffed animal contains no love, but the child does. As the little one loves the stuffed animal, love — the truth of being — is expressed, and the child feels loved. Allow the divine love that is within you to be released into the world. In this way, we echo the commandment of Jesus to: *"Love one another."*

I worked at loving for a long time, but realized that I can't perfect love. Rather, I now strive to allow myself to be vulnerable enough for God to perfect love in me. I am far off the mark when I let anger or envy take over, but I keep trying, because the greatest creativity in one's life is the capacity to allow God to inspire and to be the creative force within us.

Life is not perfect. I am not perfect, but in my imperfect way I try to remain open to God's guidance. When we turn away bitterness from filling our souls and keep fear from smothering our feelings, we allow growth to come from whatever source it might. I instinctively felt that I needed the courage to relinquish control of my life, and the faith to trust that God would take care of me. Even in the darkest moments there is a tiny wedge of light and *light always overcomes the darkness.*

Whenever I feel intimidated or fearful in a situation, I stop the intrusion long enough to ask, "in another 50 years will this really make a difference? Will I leave this legacy to bear heavily upon the lives of others should I die?" If the answer to both these questions is no, then fear loses much of its impact.

The people I appreciate most in life are those who have loved and encouraged me, affirming my sense of self-worth. I thank each of you who have helped to validate me. You have taught me more by your example than by your advice. I am wiser because of your understanding, rather than your knowledge. And you have taught me that there is greater strength in gentleness than through the assertion of power.

I learned some valuable lessons — that others gain more guidance by the quality of our interest in them than they do from all of our eminent wisdom. Each of us has a voice inside — the voice of discernment. I never force a decision. I leave it alone until the truth reveals itself, and it always does. Even a necessary snap decision can be made in confidence by trusting our intuition.

I was beginning to understand why those tiny ants of my childhood struggled so hard against the odds. They had a dream and they trusted in that dream, just as they trusted in themselves. As a child, I would lie down on a bed of moss in the forest, looking up at the tall trees, their arms outstretched. From a child's vantage point, they seemed to be holding up the sky. They were like majestic soldiers and when the breeze ruffled their strong arms, they seemed to brush the clouds from their hair. I would be as brave as those ants and as strong as those trees and I would continue to overcome the *prowling feet* — with God's help.

There will be new adventures and I will follow God's lead, probably complaining at times, but knowing that God loves me anyway. I once read a quote by Ellen Goodman that impressed me. She wrote: "It seems that this is the glue of any long-term attachment: Being Loved Anyway. Being loved anyway is not being regarded as perfect, but being accepted as imperfect."

All I ask of the world is to be loved *anyway.* And I wrote in my journal: Out of the suffering, the confusion, and the fear ... what gives us the courage to be? That I have known you and you have known me, and in the face of such terrible knowledge, we have loved each other.

Even in the midst of our troubles, we must let go of our dark moods, listen for those inner stirrings, and follow God's guidance. What makes me think God will always help me? Because I am a child of God and He is my loving Father. What more is there to say?

I've lived through many struggles and challenges in my life. As I look back, I can see more clearly the lessons that life was trying to teach me. Out of chaos often comes clarity, but it's not always transparent at the time.

Every decision we make has a cause and effect, and the consequences can bring either happiness and a successful life, or years of pain and disillusionment. Think about the consequences before venturing forward. Will they be worth it? Don't allow others to dictate whether you succeed or fail in life. If you don't take responsibility for your good decisions, someone else will take control of your life and try to pull you down, especially if you're beginning to succeed and they aren't. When people feel badly about themselves, they often want to take others with them.

Trust in God to give you answers to your daunting questions.

Stay aware of his presence and talk to him about everything — then listen for the answers. Everyone in this world has a story. Keep a journal. Write about your life and continue to look back to see the web you've woven, then discern what you did in each situation — or if another direction would have been wiser.

When we leave this world, we take with us two things: The wisdom we have gathered through the years that has helped to create who we are, and the everlasting love we hold in our hearts.

After a summer storm and the sun filters through the clouds, I am amazed to witness a rainbow painted on the sky. I no longer question the treasure awaiting me at the end of the rainbow. It's not a pot of gold. I know that when God calls me to journey across that bridge, I will have no fear, for the Lord will gather me in his arms to help me cross over. Just imagine the good Lord Himself as my companion, as I cross the bridge of love — at the other end of the rainbow.

One lesson I've learned from life:
The secret to looking back and finding the beauty
in one's life is by making today a worthy thought,
for tomorrow, it will be yesterday's memory.

So there abide faith, hope and love, these three; but the greatest of these is Love. Corinthians 13:13.

where is your brother?
husband

Made in the USA
Middletown, DE
22 February 2020

85051347R10086